THE NEW ATLATL AND DART WORKBOOK

ALSO BY WYATT R. KNAPP

The History And Primitive Technology Page
www.onagocag.com

Ongoing column and feature articles for
The Michigan Flintknappers Newsletter

The Atlatl And Dart Workbook
(with Lou Becker)

The Remarkable Fire Piston
(Society Of Primitive Technology Bulletin #38)

Writings included in
Flintknapping: Articles, Tips and Tutorials From the Internet
Compiled and edited by Michael Lynn, Cornell University:

"Below the Centerline Concept"
"Preventing Broken Points"
"Some Talk About Angles"
"Work The Ends And Then The Middle"
"Knapping On The Leg"
"Buffalo Hide As A Shock Dampening Tool"
"What Do You Really Need To Start Flintknapping?"

The Long Cold Walk
(The Detroit Free Press)

Stories Gramp Told

Descendants Of Jacob Knapp and Martha Benson

THE NEW ATLATL AND DART WORKBOOK

With 49 drawings by the author and over 60 photographs, this attractive and user-friendly book guides the reader through all the steps necessary to make a successful and effective atlatl and dart system for competition, hunting, or just plain fun. Along with redesigned atlatl plans and all new dart designs, the reader will find information and instruction on traditional hafting and fletching techniques, how to use sinew, making and attaching weights, tips on atlatl mechanics and how they effect dart performance, and more. THE NEW ATLATL AND DART WORKBOOK is a valuable reference and resource for both beginning and more knowledgeable atlatl enthusiasts.

THE ATLATL AND DART WORKBOOK

"... if you have an atlatl part of your library, this book will most definitely need to be there!"

-Gary L. Fogelman, Editor, *Indian Artifact Magazine*

"... a wonderful, information-packed book, great format, and very reader friendly."

-Sue Harrison, Author of *Mother Earth Father Sky,* Storyteller Trilogy, and the Ivory Carver Trilogy.

"... this book is for those who want to rediscover the joy of the atlatl... if you are interested in building one this book will instruct on how to do it and do it well... it is well and clearly written... if you feel the urge to build one, this is the book for you."

-Gene Langston, Editor, *Primitive Archer Magazine*

"... a well thought out work ... describing to the reader how to make an effective atlatl system that really works... "

-Bill Tate, Editor, *The Atlatl,* official newsletter of *The World Atlatl Association.*

THE HISTORY AND PRIMITIVE TECHNOLOGY PAGE

Recipient of the University of California at Santa Barbara's "Cool Site" award.

"... [The History And Primitive Technology Page] has been judged to contain quality content, design and/or HTML expertise."

-Ravi's Elite Site Award

"... a good starting place... to learn about humanity's most primitive survival skills... with articles on ancient fire-making machines, flintknapping, buckskinning, and the secrets of the deadly atlatl, or dart thrower. The author of the site, Wyatt R. Knapp, is quick to point out that 'primitive' means earliest or original; it 'does not mean less intelligent, or less creative, or less inventive.'"

-Natural History Magazine

<u>IMPORTANT SAFETY NOTICE</u>:

Always keep safety foremost in mind. If you make any of the projects in this book, be advised that the author, publisher, and bookseller are NOT responsible for your safety. Any projects you make as described herein are to be used at your own risk. Read and follow the safety guidelines found on Page Three of this book.

THE NEW ATLATL AND DART WORKBOOK

HOW TO MAKE YOUR OWN ATLATL AND DARTS FOR COMPETITION, HUNTING, AND FUN

WYATT R. KNAPP

ILLUSTRATED BY WYATT R. KNAPP

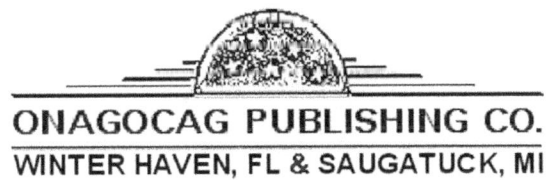

ONAGOCAG PUBLISHING CO.
WINTER HAVEN, FL & SAUGATUCK, MI

"OH-NAH-GO-SHOG"

CONTENTS

ACKNOWLEDGMENTS

I wish to acknowledge and thank:

All those friends who over the years shared their knowledge of primitive skills and methods. There are too many to mention, but if I did, among them would be John Geyer, Dan Belknap, Don Gilson, Clay Wykes, Chris Oberg, Kevin Finney and Jerry Ulrich.

My dad, who gave me my love of history, American Indian lore, and primitive technology. I'd also like to thank my mom, an author herself, for so generously giving of her time and expertise. Thanks, Mom and Dad, for always encouraging me and supporting my interests, my art and my writing, and for instilling at an early age a curiosity about the world around me.

And finally, my beautiful wife Shari, who tirelessly worked at my side as co-editor. She contributed in other areas as well, from inking drawing outlines, to photography, to page layouts and more. Thank you, Shari. You shared my love for this project and encouraged me to keep going through long hours and many revisions. And you throw a mean atlatl dart too!

INTRODUCTION

Many sources have documented the chilling effect the atlatl had on the conquistadors who accompanied Cortez on his trek through Mexico in 1520 A.D. Surely the Spanish felt they were the better equipped state-of-the-art military machine. The armies Cortez brought with him to the New World represented the height of armored splendor and firearm technology for the times. They were in a position to make a dramatic statement to the natives that would demonstrate just what that machine could do. But it would not be that simple. Instead they met with a terrifying stone-age technology--the atlatl and dart.

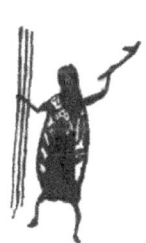

The atlatl and dart system consists of a wooden thrower or handle (the atlatl) which is about two feet long. At the tip end is a hook or point. The second part, the dart, is like a really long arrow. It is hollowed out a bit at the back end so that it fits on the hook of the thrower. The dart is then cast from the atlatl. An atlatl in the hands of an expert can throw a dart accurately enough to hit a target one hundred yards away.

Cortez's soldiers learned that in addition to the long-range capability of this weapon, the points on the six-foot-long darts were barbed and had to be drawn out the other side to be removed. This made for a slow and agonizing death. You can well imagine the terror exacted on these men.

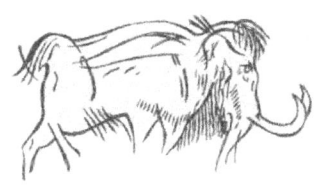

But long before the arrival of Cortez, back in prehistoric times, the earliest settlers of the Americas were faced with dangers of another sort. Things like "dire wolves" that were five or six times the size of the wolves of today. And they liked to snack on people. The atlatl provided an effective means of survival as it was useful in repelling and killing these and other predatory animals.

The atlatl was the main hunting tool for well over 12,000 years in the Americas before being replaced by the bow and arrow around 2,000 BC. There are those who place its use in Europe to as much as 30,000 years ago. Its dependability and effectiveness as a hunting weapon is thought to have been a major contributing factor in the extinction of much of the mega-fauna in the Americas including animals like the mastodon and woolly mammoth.

Early attempts at recreating an effective atlatl and dart system weren't very successful and many scholars doubted the stories told by the conquistadors. Those who tried to use these early designs were somewhat disappointed in their performance because the darts were too heavy, making them more like spears, and their atlatl designs were often too short and more like flat baseball bats.

The word "atlatl" is from the Nahuatl language spoken by the Aztecs. In an interview with a Nahuatl professor, I learned the word is pronounced "aht-laht-ull", with the emphasis on the first syllable. An alternate pronunciation would be "at-latt-ell".

After decades of research we have a better understanding of how the system functions and can now boast of atlatls and darts that perform like those of the ancients. We are a far cry from the early days when only a handful of people were throwing darts. There has been a tremendous surge of interest. Dart throwing has become an international sport with tournaments held in the United States and abroad. Many of these tournaments are held under the auspices of the World Atlatl Association which was formed in 1987 to organize and promote the sport.

Today atlatls are used for hunting, fishing, in competition, and just for the sheer enjoyment of launching the powerful darts into the air and watching them gracefully sail far downfield. Interest in the atlatl is booming. Now is the perfect time to learn about atlatls and darts, to make them, and be part of the fun!

The Objective Of This Book

With the heightened interest and growing number of atlatl enthusiasts out there, we can naturally expect there are going to be plenty of ideas about how to make a successful atlatl and dart 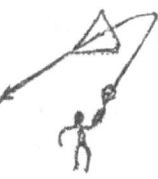 system. There are aspects of atlatl and dart 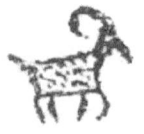 construction that are hotly debated. Some say both the atlatl and dart need to be flexible. Others say only the dart has to flex. Some say the atlatl has to be matched to a person's arm length, or that the fletching on the darts or weights on the atlatl aren't needed. Then you will talk to some who insist they are quite necessary. Even the function of the weights on an atlatl is debated.

The variety of designs being used and sold can be daunting to the contemporary atlatlist. Some are very good, but some are designed poorly, giving the average person a false impression about the effectiveness of the system. With all the designs and different ideas out there about making atlatls and darts, how do you plow through them and come up with something you can use with confidence?

That's where *The New Atlatl And Dart Workbook* comes in. It will show you how to make a truly effective atlatl and dart system, whether you are looking to compete, hunt or just have fun! In this book you will benefit from years of atlatl and dart experimentation and manufacturing experience. What you'll get here is straight information, measured drawings and complete instructions for making your own atlatls and darts, along with pictures to help illustrate the process. In addition, you'll find information on hunting, fishing, and competing as well as some games you can play to develop skill and accuracy.

The designs shared in this book are proven successes. They are dependable tools for use in hunting and fishing situations and have been used to win prizes in competition. The designs have been employed with great satisfaction all over the world. Making an atlatl and darts according to the instructions in this book will provide you with a professional, highly effective working system you will be proud to own. When you use them you can concentrate on practicing and becoming proficient at the sport. You won't have to worry that your equipment is hindering your progress.

Although some modern tools, materials and adhesives are used in this book, you will find most of the designs lend themselves to the use of stone-age materials and methods as well.

AN IMPORTANT WORD ABOUT SAFETY!!

Before we get into the assembly instructions we need to talk about safety. The atlatl and dart system is a deadly weapon. In this chapter you've read about how effective it was for hunting and defense. Many of the stories told about its penetration capabilities are true. Under the right conditions an atlatl dart will pierce the metal wall of a pole barn. It has a range of over 145 yards, and the power of the dart, when using steel broadheads or flint dart points, is sufficient to kill an elephant.

You need to use the same precautions you would with archery or firearms. Give yourself plenty of room and be aware of your surroundings. Never allow children to throw darts with the atlatl unless they are under close adult supervision. Establish a safety line behind the person throwing darts and keep all people and animals well behind it. Do not throw darts if there are people or animals ahead of the safety line. Sometimes when throwing for distance, the dart can get a little kick from a tail wind and sail farther than you thought it would. But if you regard it as a weapon, and use care, you'll find it quite safe. Continued practice will increase your skills, and you will experience greater enjoyment and satisfaction whenever you are engaged in this unique and healthful sport.

Now… let's make an atlatl and some darts!

Remember:

- *Keep safety foremost in mind*

- *Give yourself plenty of room and be aware of your surroundings*

- *Never allow children to use the atlatl without close adult supervision*

- *Establish a safety line behind the person throwing darts*

- *Keep all people and animals behind the safety line*

ATLATLS

PRIMITIVE STYLE ATLATL

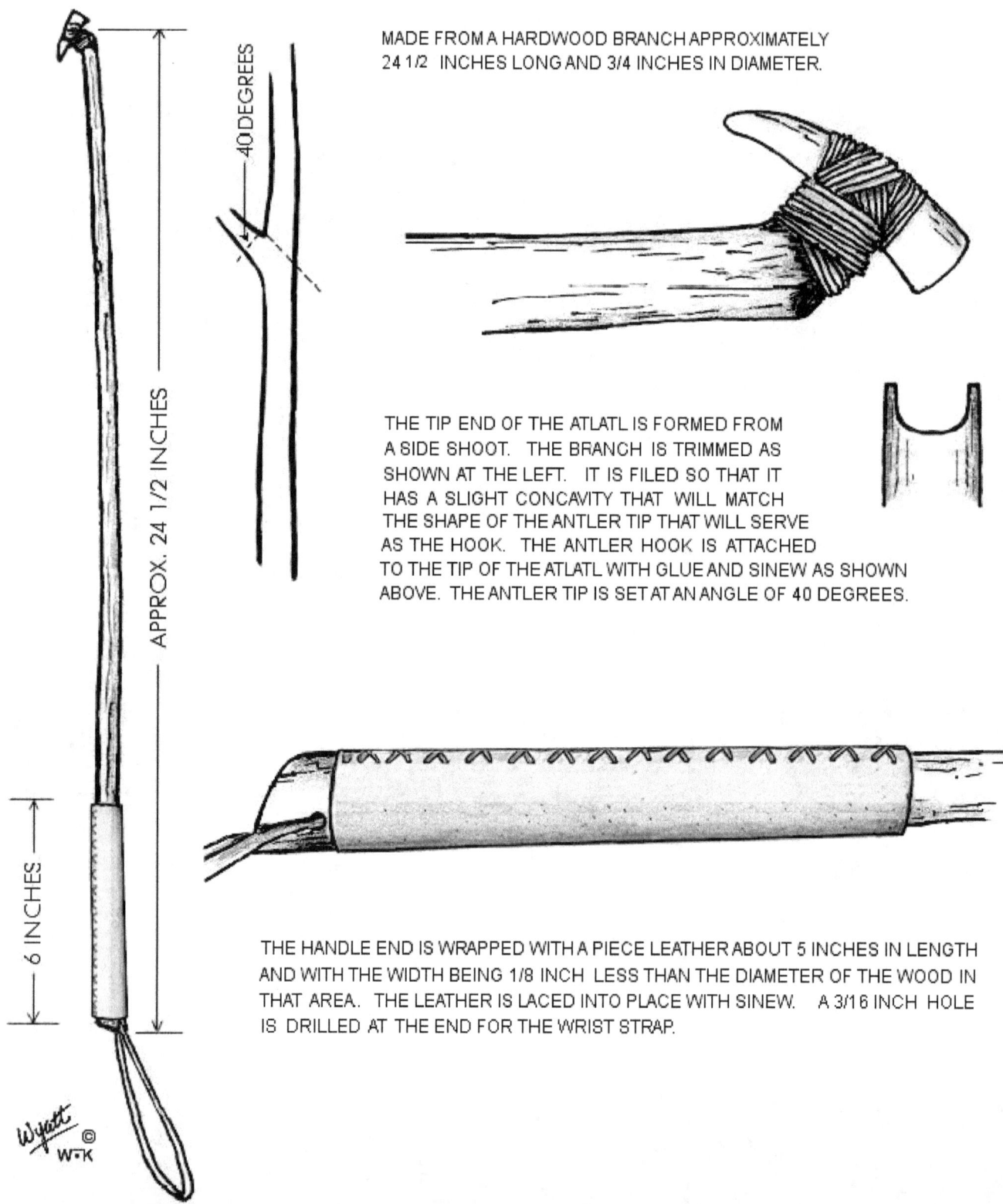

MADE FROM A HARDWOOD BRANCH APPROXIMATELY
24 1/2 INCHES LONG AND 3/4 INCHES IN DIAMETER.

THE TIP END OF THE ATLATL IS FORMED FROM
A SIDE SHOOT.   THE BRANCH IS TRIMMED AS
SHOWN AT THE LEFT.   IT IS FILED SO THAT IT
HAS A SLIGHT CONCAVITY THAT WILL MATCH
THE SHAPE OF THE ANTLER TIP THAT WILL SERVE
AS THE HOOK.   THE ANTLER HOOK IS ATTACHED
TO THE TIP OF THE ATLATL WITH GLUE AND SINEW AS SHOWN
ABOVE. THE ANTLER TIP IS SET AT AN ANGLE OF 40 DEGREES.

THE HANDLE END IS WRAPPED WITH A PIECE LEATHER ABOUT 5 INCHES IN LENGTH
AND WITH THE WIDTH BEING 1/8 INCH LESS THAN THE DIAMETER OF THE WOOD IN
THAT AREA.   THE LEATHER IS LACED INTO PLACE WITH SINEW.   A 3/16 INCH HOLE
IS DRILLED AT THE END FOR THE WRIST STRAP.

40 DEGREES

APPROX. 24 1/2 INCHES

6 INCHES

Wyatt ©
W-K

6

PRIMITIVE STYLE ATLATL

Here's an atlatl you can make styled much like the ones that may have been used 12,000 years ago. Although at first glance it appears to be a simple weapon, don't be fooled. Primitive atlatls incorporated all the physics necessary to bring down mighty mastodons, woolly mammoths, and other mega fauna. It was a highly effective hunting tool that literally changed the face of the Americas.

The beauty of this atlatl is in its rustic look. The natural bark of the wood is retained and accentuated by golden sinew wrappings and a smooth antler hook. This is a fully functional thrower you will enjoy using and displaying.

PARTS

MAIN SHAFT

The main shaft is 24-½ inches long (62.23 cm) and about 3/4 inches in diameter (1.905 cm) at the handle end and is made out of a branch from a hardwood tree. Any hardwood will work, but a smoother bark is best as it has a nicer appearance and won't peel. Maple is a good choice as is hickory. The example shown here was made of oak.

The branch does not have to be perfectly straight. It can have some character. Look for one with a small crook or branch at the narrower end that can serve as a base on which to attach the hook. Use the drawings on the left as a reference. There's no need to wait for the wood to season or dry.

LEATHER HANDLE WRAP

Measure the diameter of the main shaft of the branch at the handle end and subtract 1/8 inch. This is the measurement for the width of the leather strip. The measurement for the length is 5 inches.

ANTLER HOOK

The hook is the part of the atlatl that engages the dart. It needs to be made of a durable, smooth material so it can stand up to the pressures of use and give the dart a smooth release. The hook for our primitive style atlatl is made from the tip of a deer antler tine but you can also use antler material from moose or elk.

LATIGO LACE WRIST STRAP

For the wrist strap, a length of real leather latigo lacing (or leather shoe lacing) works well. Be sure to make it long enough to fit over the wrist comfortably.

SINEW

Historically sinew was used for sewing, making moccasins, attaching arrowheads to shafts, etc. because it's a very tough binding material. It is found in the legs and along the back of deer, moose and elk. Although many people prefer real sinew, some find it more convenient to use artificial sinew. If care is taken in choosing a brand it can look quite authentic. If you decide to use artificial sinew, look for something slightly transparent with a nice golden color, and give it a coating of beeswax before using. But the look and strength of real sinew are hard to beat. For instructions on using real sinew, refer to Page 77 in the Appendix.

ASSEMBLY

STEP ONE: PREPARE THE BRANCH

Cut the branch to a length of 24 ½ inches (62.23 cm). Trim off any twigs or branches. Shape the tip end so the knob left over from where the side branch was attached provides a platform for attaching the antler tip. The mating surface for the antler tip should be slightly concave so as to fit the shape of the tip. It should allow for the tip to rest at a 45 degree angle. (See drawings on Page 6.) Using a wood rasp, smooth out any bumps from where twigs were trimmed.

STEP TWO: THE WRIST STRAP

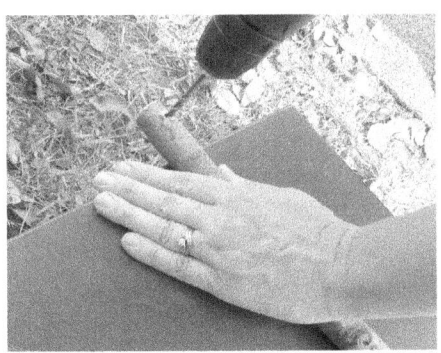

Drill a 3/16 inch hole at the back end of the body as indicated in the drawing. This will be used for attaching the wrist strap. Pass one end of the latigo lacing through the hole in the handle end of the atlatl. Pull it through until it's even with the other end of the lacing and tie it off. You can leave the ends extra long and add pony beads for decoration if you wish.

STEP THREE: LEATHER HANDLE WRAP

Using a leather punch or an awl, make 20 equally spaced holes along both of the 5 inch edges of the rectangle of leather. Using sinew, loosely sew the two sides of the leather together around the handle as if you were lacing up a shoe. When you reach the last set of holes, pull the sinew tight so as to close up the gap. The leather should fit very tightly around the handle--you should not be able to turn it or slip it off. It is best to end up with the sinew coming out from under the leather wrap and then to tie it off, leaving about an inch of sinew beyond the knots. Tuck the knots and extra sinew underneath and out of sight with the careful use of a screwdriver, if needed.

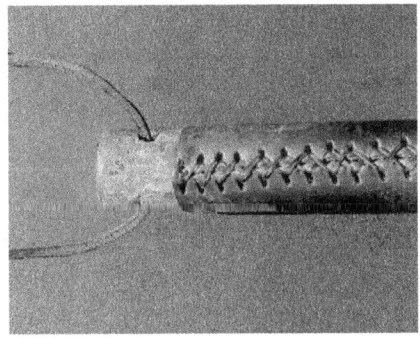

STEP FOUR: ATTACHING THE ANTLER HOOK

Apply epoxy to the hook and secure it to the tip of the atlatl. Make several tight wraps of sinew to secure it in place as shown in the drawing on Page 6. As you apply the wraps, use your thumb to hold the tip at the proper angle of 40 degrees. The hook should also be aligned with the center of the body of the atlatl. Add several more tight wrappings, checking the angle and alignment frequently. Tie off the end of the sinew and set aside to dry. (Refer to the Appendix for instructions on using and tying off sinew.)

STEP FIVE: FINISHING

Sand the atlatl with fine sandpaper. Treat the end with tung oil to prevent checking. If you used a smooth barked wood, finish the entire branch with the oil to heighten the grain and color. Now you can take some time to look over your atlatl and admire your handiwork. Pretty neat, isn't it?

So…what would you like to do next? Maybe you'd like to add some finger loops. They'd look great and give you a more secure and consistent grip (See Page 80.) Or, you could continue on to the instructions for making "The Classic Hunting Atlatl". Maybe you'd rather turn to the Darts section and find one you'd like to make so you can start throwing right away!

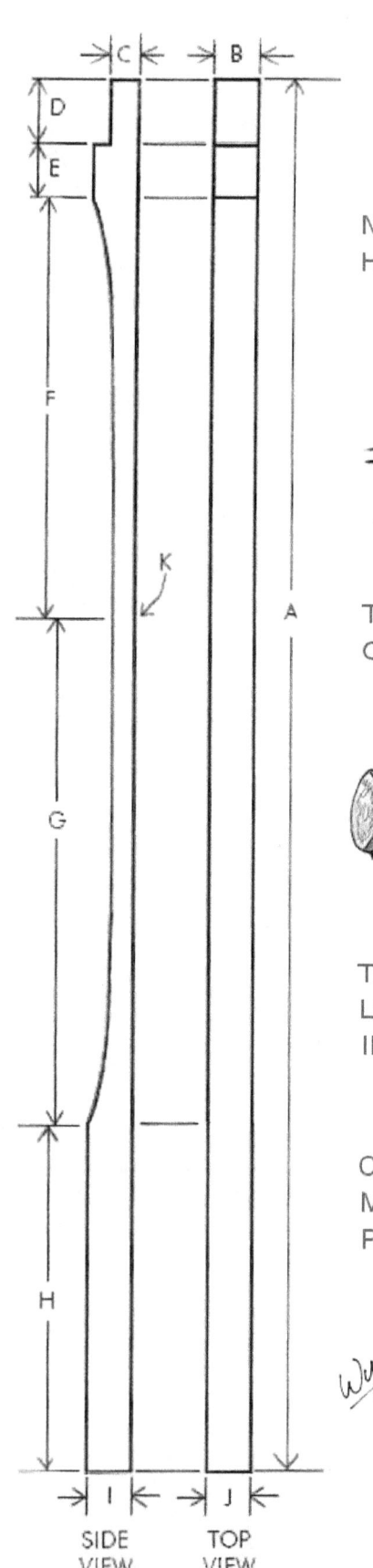

CLASSIC HUNTING ATLATL

MADE FROM A 24 INCH LONG, 3/4 INCH DIAMETER HARDWOOD DOWEL

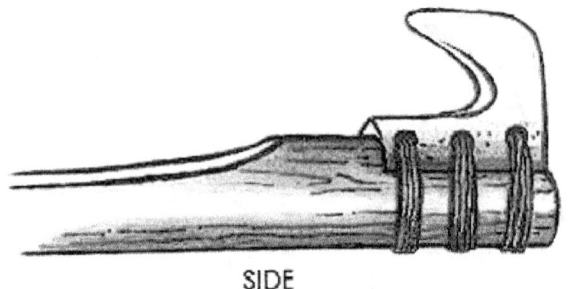
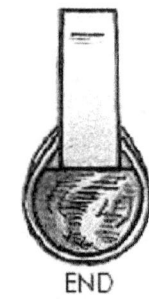

SIDE   END

THE HOOK IS GLUED AND THEN SECURED TO THE END OF THE ATLATL WITH WRAPPINGS OF SINEW

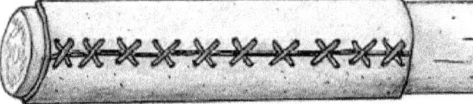

TOP

THE HANDLE END IS WRAPPED WITH A SQUARE OF LEATHER WHICH IS SECURED WITH SINEW AS SHOWN IN THE DRAWING ABOVE

CONSIDER ADDING FINGER LOOPS TO THIS DESIGN FOR A MORE SECURE AND CONSISTENT GRIP. (SEE APPENDIX, PAGE 78)

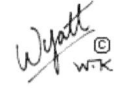

DIMENSIONS	
A = 24 INCHES (60.96 cm)	F = 8 INCHES (20.32 cm)
B = 3/4 INCH (1.905 cm)	G = 8 INCHES (20.32 cm)
C = 1/2 INCH (1.27 cm)	H = 6 INCHES (15.24 cm)
D = 1 1/4 INCHES (3.175 cm)	I = 3/4 INCH (1.905 cm)
E = 3/4 INCH (1.905 cm)	J = 3/4 INCH (1.905 cm)

THE HEIGHT OF THE SHAFT AT "K" IS 1/2 INCH (1.27 cm)

CLASSIC HUNTING ATLATL

Although this attractive atlatl is more contemporary in nature than the Primitive Style Atlatl, its design retains age-old features, and the use of natural materials gives it a very authentic look. The Classic Hunting Atlatl is designed to fit comfortably and securely in the hand. This style of atlatl has not only been used to take trophies and prizes in competition, but has also been used with great success in hunting situations to take wild boar, white-tailed deer, and African game animals. This atlatl is a durable and consistent performer that has helped many a beginner reach new levels in competition and sporting accuracy.

PARTS

BODY

The body is made out of ¾ inch (1.905 cm) hardwood dowel stock. Avoid using softer woods like pine and basswood. It is better to use hardwoods such as maple, oak and walnut. The example shown here was made of osage orange.

ANTLER HOOK

The hook on this atlatl was made out of moose antler. An alternative for using real antler is a man-made material called "UHMW" (Ultra High Molecular Weight). It's a nylon plastic material sold in ½ inch thick sheets. Although it is super hard and durable, it can be worked easily with hand tools. You can use X-Acto® knives and coping saws to carve and cut it.

LEATHER HANDLE WRAP

A rectangle of leather measuring 5 inches by about 3 ¾ inches.

CLASSIC HUNTING ATLATL
PATTERNS

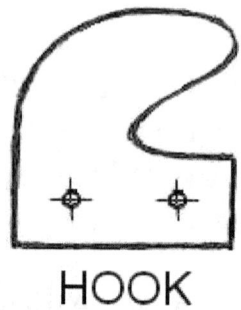

HOOK

(SHOWN FULL SIZE)

THE HOOK CAN BE SAWN USING A BANDSAW
OR COPING SAW. IT IS THEN BROUGHT TO ITS
FINAL SHAPE USING FILES FOR HOOKS MADE
OF ANTLER, OR AN X-ACTO® KNIFE IF YOU
USE UHDW MATERIAL.

WEIGHT

(OPTIONAL)
SHOWN FULL SIZE

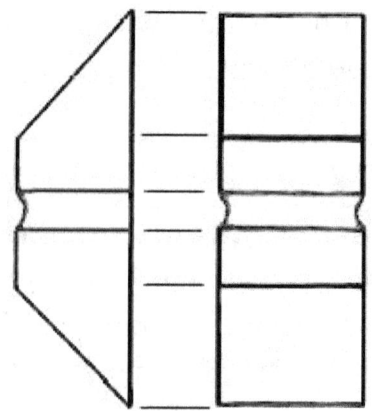

IF YOU WISH TO ADD A WEIGHT TO YOUR
ATLATL, TRY ONE MADE OF CARVING STONE
OR SOAPSTONE USING THE DRAWING ABOVE
AS A REFERENCE.   ADJUST THE SIZE TO
ALLOW FOR ENOUGH STONE TO BRING IT
TO THE CORRECT WEIGHT WHEN FINISHED.
THE GROOVE IS TO HOLD THE SINEW WRAP
IN PLACE WHEN TYING IT TO THE ATLATL.

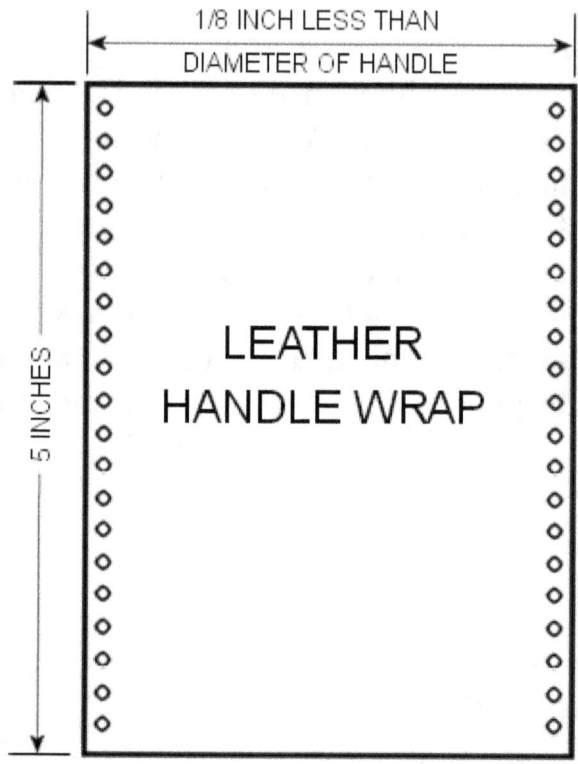

1/8 INCH LESS THAN
DIAMETER OF HANDLE

5 INCHES

LEATHER
HANDLE WRAP

CONVERSIONS

1/8 INCHES = .3175 CM
3 3/4 INCHES = 9.525 CM
5 INCHES = 12.7 CM

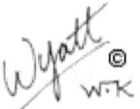

WEIGHT: (Optional)

Original weights on ancient atlatls were made of various types of stone, including soapstone and slate. Atlatl weights seem to be a wholly North American phenomenon. Evidence for their use elsewhere in the world has yet to be found. As we mentioned in the Introduction of this workbook, there is plenty of debate over the use of weights on the atlatl. It is thought by many that when the atlatl "turns over" during use, the inertia from the mass of the weight transfers to the dart, giving it more cast. Some feel atlatl weights help as a counter balance for the weight of a dart when loaded onto the thrower. Yet other researchers believe weights were used merely for ornamental or ceremonial purposes. You may have read about huge atlatl weights as part of the archaeological record. (Some of these specimens weigh as much as 1,000 grams.) The purpose of these heavy weights is unclear. Recent studies have shown that weights in excess of 50 grams tend to impede atlatl performance rather than improve it. Use of excessively heavy weights can also lead to painful injury of your shoulder, elbow or arm.

If you decide to add a weight to this atlatl design, it should weigh approximately 1 to 1-1/2 ounces (about 30-45 grams). If you don't have a small scale available, keep in mind that a U.S. nickel weighs 5 grams.

SINEW

Artificial or real sinew can be used. (See Appendix for instructions on using and tying sinew.)

ASSEMBLY

STEP ONE: MAKING THE HOOK

Saw the shape of the hook out of moose horn using a band saw or coping saw according to the pattern given in the drawing on Page 14. If you decide to use UHMW material you can use an X-Acto® knife to shape it. Drill two or three lashing holes in the bottom edge as shown in the pattern using a 3/16 inch drill. Don't worry about getting the point shape exactly right yet as it will be addressed in Step Four.

STEP TWO: DESIGN LAYOUT AND MAKING THE NOTCH

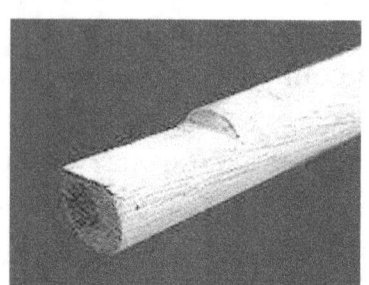

Use a pencil to mark the guidelines onto the wood shaft as indicated in the drawing. The notch is 1 ¼ inches long and ¼ inch deep. Use a coping saw to carefully make some kerfs which will serve as a guide for the chisel. With the bevel side down, use the chisel to remove the wood from the notch. (Working with the bevel side down helps to keep you from digging too deeply into the wood.)   Next, use a rasp to smooth the bottom of the notch. Test the fit of the mating surfaces between the hook and the atlatl shaft and adjust with filing if necessary.

STEP THREE: SHAPING THE BELLY OF THE SHAFT

Using a draw knife or wood rasp, shape the belly of the atlatl by making a shallow concavity ½ inch deep at the mid-point and tapered up so it blends into the top of the shaft at both ends as shown in the drawing on Page 12. (If you have the skill, an alternative would be to carefully cut out the shape of the belly with a band saw.)   Don't go too deep or you may compromise the stability of the shaft. After the shaping is done, smooth out the areas with a wood rasp. Finally, remove all of the tool marks by scraping with a draw knife or cabinet scraper.

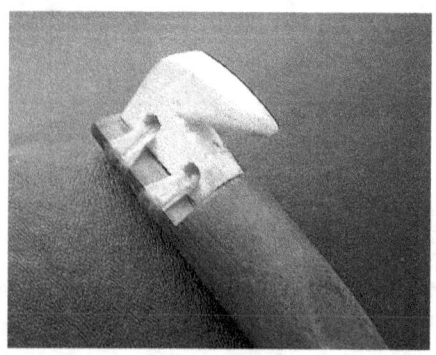

STEP FOUR: ATTACHING THE HOOK TO THE ATLATL SHAFT

Begin by using epoxy to glue the hook in place on the atlatl shaft. Check the hook to make sure it's properly aligned and centered in relation to the shaft of the atlatl. Doing so will provide a proper and accurate release for the dart. Set aside to dry.

Using fairly long pieces of sinew, lash the hook to the shaft as shown in the pictures. It's as if you were sewing the hook onto the atlatl. When everything is dry and tight you can do the final shaping of the hook to make sure it matches the examples in the pictures and drawings.

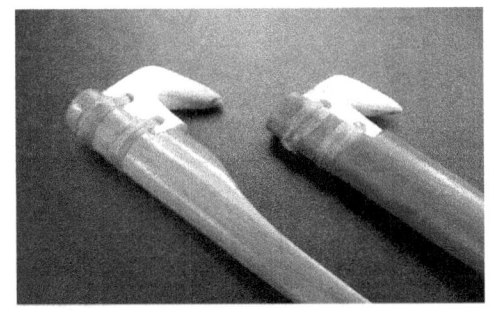

STEP FIVE: FINAL SANDING AND APPLYING FINISH TO THE ATLATL

Sand the entire body of the atlatl using rough sandpaper first, then medium. Remove all tool and pencil marks. Next apply rubbing alcohol to the body of the atlatl in order to raise the grain. Follow with a pass of fine sandpaper. Raise the grain again and sand with very fine sandpaper. You may continue raising the grain and sanding with fine sandpaper until you get the smoothness you desire. Apply a coating of the clear lacquer to the atlatl. Hang it up to dry until it's ready for another coat. Apply a second coat of lacquer and allow it to dry.

STEP SIX: LEATHER HANDLE WRAP

Using a leather punch or an awl, make 20 equally spaced holes along both of the 5 inch edges of the rectangle of leather. Using sinew, loosely sew the two sides of the leather together around the handle as if you were lacing up a shoe. When you reach the last set of holes, pull the sinew tight so as to close up the gap. The leather should fit very tightly around the handle--you should not be able to turn it or slip it off. It is best to end up with the sinew coming out from under the leather wrap and then to tie it off, leaving about an inch of sinew beyond the knots. Tuck the knots and extra sinew underneath and out of sight with the careful use of a screwdriver, if needed.

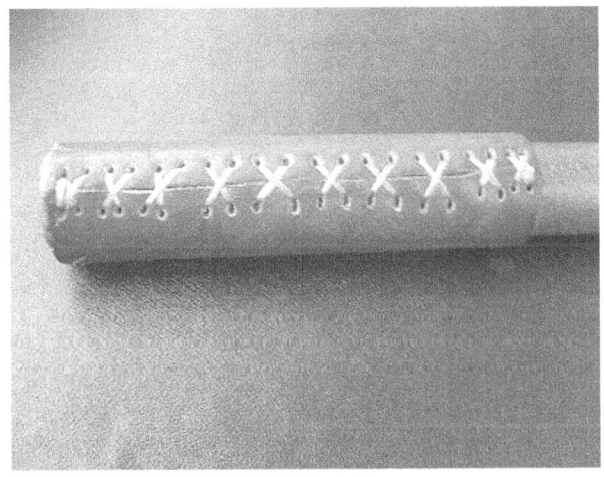

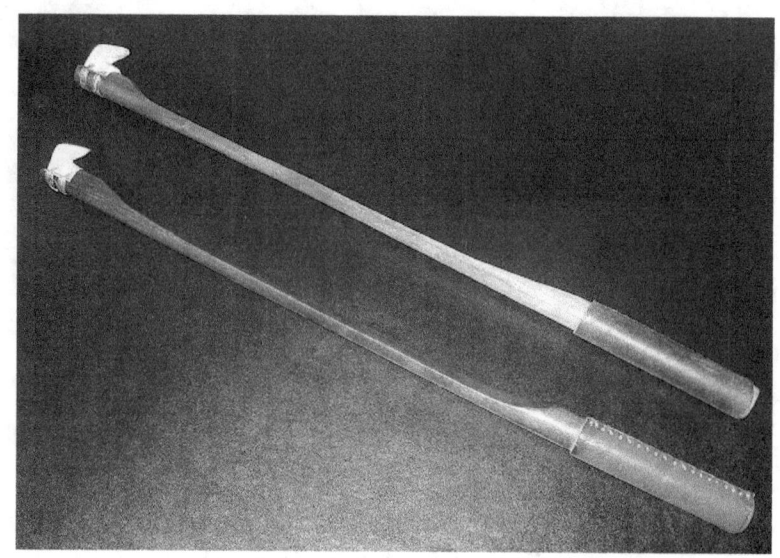

Pictured At Right:

Two finished Classic Hunting Atlatls. Leather finger loops matched to the color of the handle wraps may be added if desired. (See Pages 80-81 in the Appendix.)

STEP SEVEN: ADDING A WEIGHT (OPTIONAL)

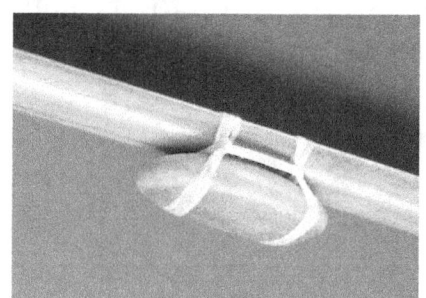

You can use a custom shaped soapstone weight as described in the Parts list for this Classic Hunting Atlatl and shown on the full page drawing found on Page 14. Or, if you prefer, you can simply find a flat oval-shaped stone of the recommended weight and tie it onto the atlatl using sinew wraps as shown. Both methods are equally authentic.

Placement of the weight varies with different styles of atlatls. You can experiment with its placement by securely attaching it using duct tape. Field test it with the weight taped in various places on the atlatl until you find a position that feels comfortable and works best for you. For this particular atlatl design, it seems to work well about 6 or 7 inches ahead of the handle wrap.

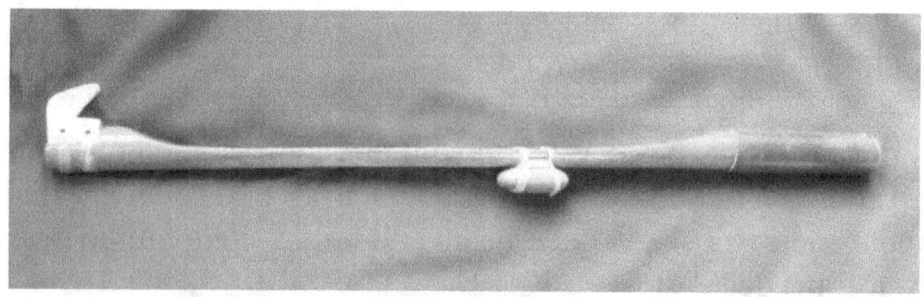

THE FLEXIBLE STYLE ATLATL

The flexible atlatl has its share of admirers, and it is felt by many that the spring energy it provides works in conjunction with the spring energy of the dart to improve the power of the system. Bob Perkins of BPS Engineering has done much research in this area, and is arguably the most ardent promoter of the flexible atlatl and dart system.

On the following pages you will find plans for two types of flexible atlatls. The first is reminiscent of the Basketmaker style atlatl. The second incorporates contemporary features into a simple and clean design. Given your experience with the previous plans in this book, you shouldn't have any trouble following the instructions as given here. Don't be afraid to experiment a little with the lengths and designs.

As you attend more and more atlatl gatherings, you're likely to meet someone who has made the best of an unfortunate situation. You see, many a broken bow has been pressed into service as a flexible style atlatl.

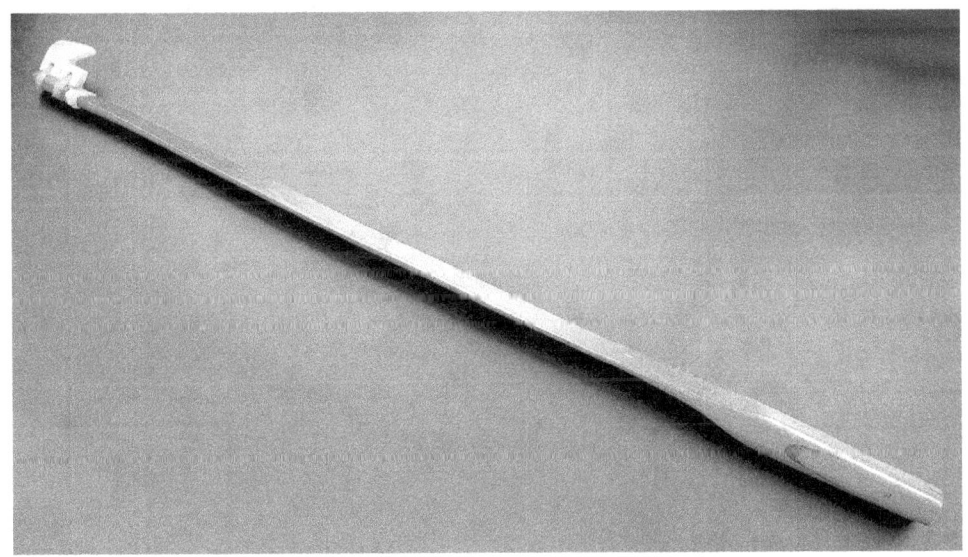

Atlatl made by the author from a broken bow

CONTEMPORARY BASKETMAKER
STYLE ATLATL

A CONTEMPORARY ATLATL WITH TRADITIONAL BASKETMAKER FEATURES. MAKE IT
FROM A GOOD FLEXIBLE WOOD LIKE HICKORY OR OSAGE. IF IT WILL MAKE A BOW IT
WILL WORK FOR THIS ATLATL.

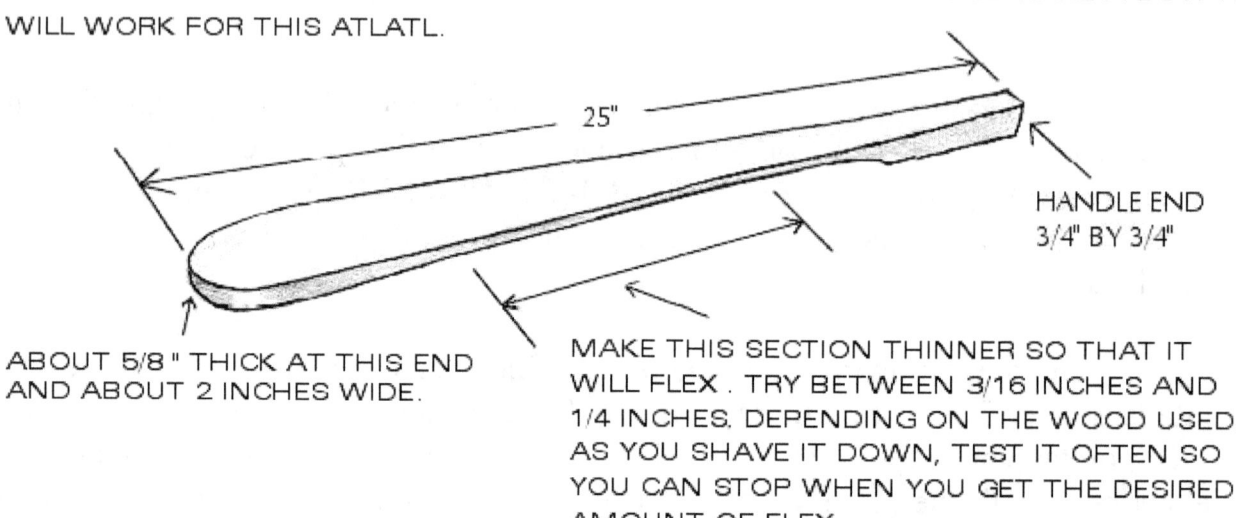

25"

HANDLE END
3/4" BY 3/4"

ABOUT 5/8 " THICK AT THIS END
AND ABOUT 2 INCHES WIDE.

MAKE THIS SECTION THINNER SO THAT IT
WILL FLEX . TRY BETWEEN 3/16 INCHES AND
1/4 INCHES. DEPENDING ON THE WOOD USED.
AS YOU SHAVE IT DOWN, TEST IT OFTEN SO
YOU CAN STOP WHEN YOU GET THE DESIRED
AMOUNT OF FLEX.

A SHALLOW CHANNEL IS GOUGED
OUT WITH A CHISEL. BLEND THE
POINTED END INTO THE TOP OF
THE ATLATL.

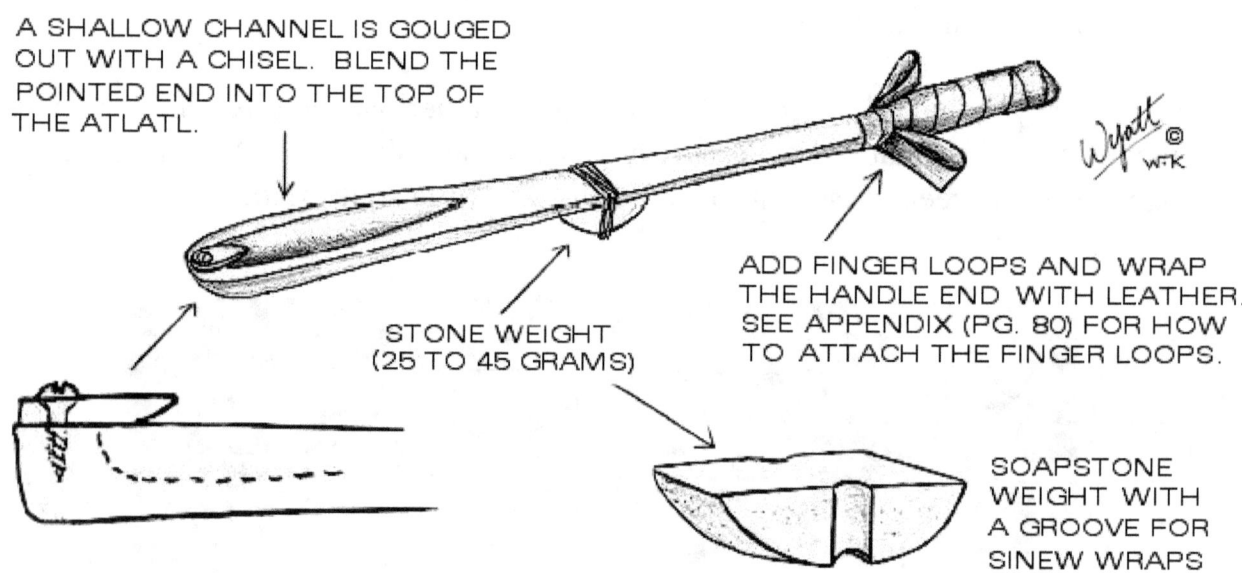

STONE WEIGHT
(25 TO 45 GRAMS)

ADD FINGER LOOPS AND WRAP
THE HANDLE END WITH LEATHER.
SEE APPENDIX (PG. 80) FOR HOW
TO ATTACH THE FINGER LOOPS.

SOAPSTONE
WEIGHT WITH
A GROOVE FOR
SINEW WRAPS

MAKE THE SPUR FROM A PIECE OF ANTLER.
EPOXY IT TO THE ATLATL AS SHOWN AND
THEN USE A SMALL SCREW OR WOODEN PEG
TO FURTHER SECURE IT. OR YOU COULD CARVE
THE SPUR INTO WOOD AS PART OF THE
CHANNEL.

SAND IT REAL SMOOTH USING VARIOUS
GRADES OF SANDPAPER. FINISH WITH
SHELLAC OR A FEW COATS OF FURNITURE
WAX AND RUB IT DOWN TO A NICE LUSTER.

CONVERSIONS
2 INCHES = 5.08 CM
5/8 INCHES = 1.587 CM
3/4 INCHES = 1.905 CM
25 INCHES = 63.5 CM

A SECOND FLEXIBLE ATLATL

ONCE AGAIN, A GOOD FLEXIBLE WOOD LIKE HICKORY OR OSAGE IS RECOMMENDED.

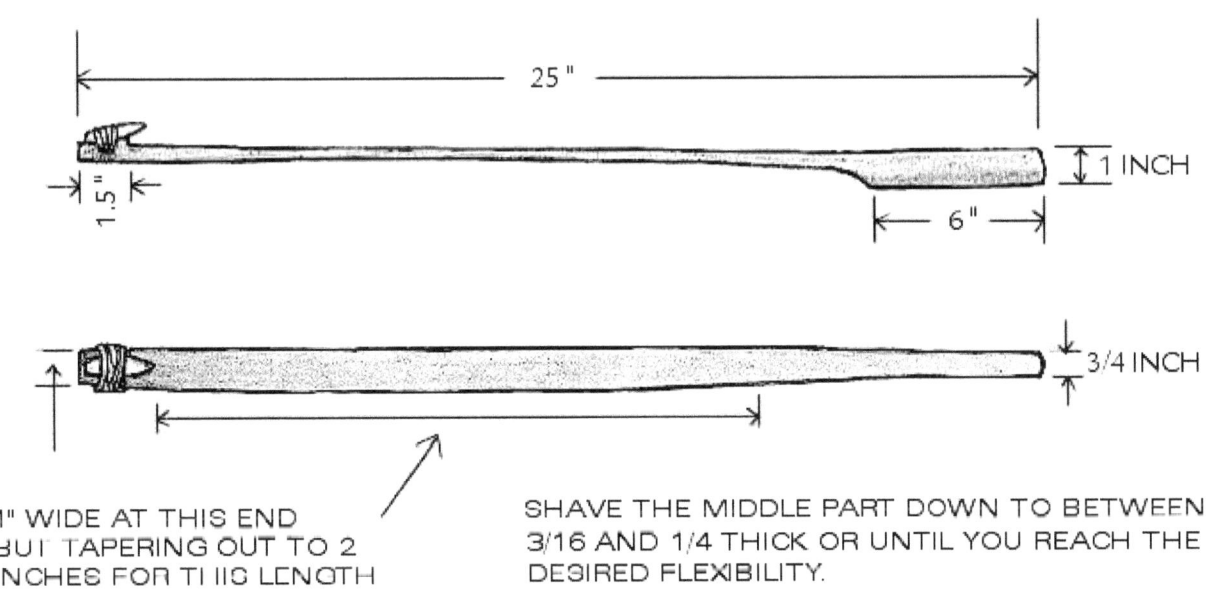

1" WIDE AT THIS END
BUT TAPERING OUT TO 2
INCHES FOR THIS LENGTH

SHAVE THE MIDDLE PART DOWN TO BETWEEN
3/16 AND 1/4 THICK OR UNTIL YOU REACH THE
DESIRED FLEXIBILITY.

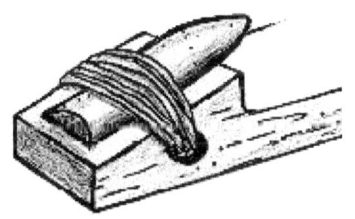

THE TIP END IS SHAPED AS SHOWN. THE HOOK IS MADE
FROM A HORN TIP FROM A DEER ANTLER. THE ANTLER
TIP IS SAWED IN HALF LENGTHWISE AND THEN EPOXIED
TO THE 40 DEGREE INCLINE OF THE END. THE HOOK ON
THIS ATLATL IS FURTHER SECURED WITH WRAPS OF
SINEW.

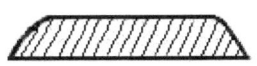

HERE'S A DRAWING OF A CROSS SECTION OF THE
ATLATL AT ABOUT THE MIDPOINT. YOU CAN SEE
THAT THE TOP EDGES HAVE BEEN ROUNDED OVER
BUT THE BOTTOM REMAINS FLAT. THIS FLAT
BOTTOM MAKES IT EASIER TO SECURE A WEIGHT
IF YOU DESIRE.

Wyatt ©
W-K

CONVERSIONS
3/16 INCHES = .476 CM
3/4 INCHES = 1.905 CM
1 INCH = 2.54 CM
1.5 INCHES = 3.81 CM
6 INCHES = 15.24 CM
25 INCHES = 63.5 CM

DARTS

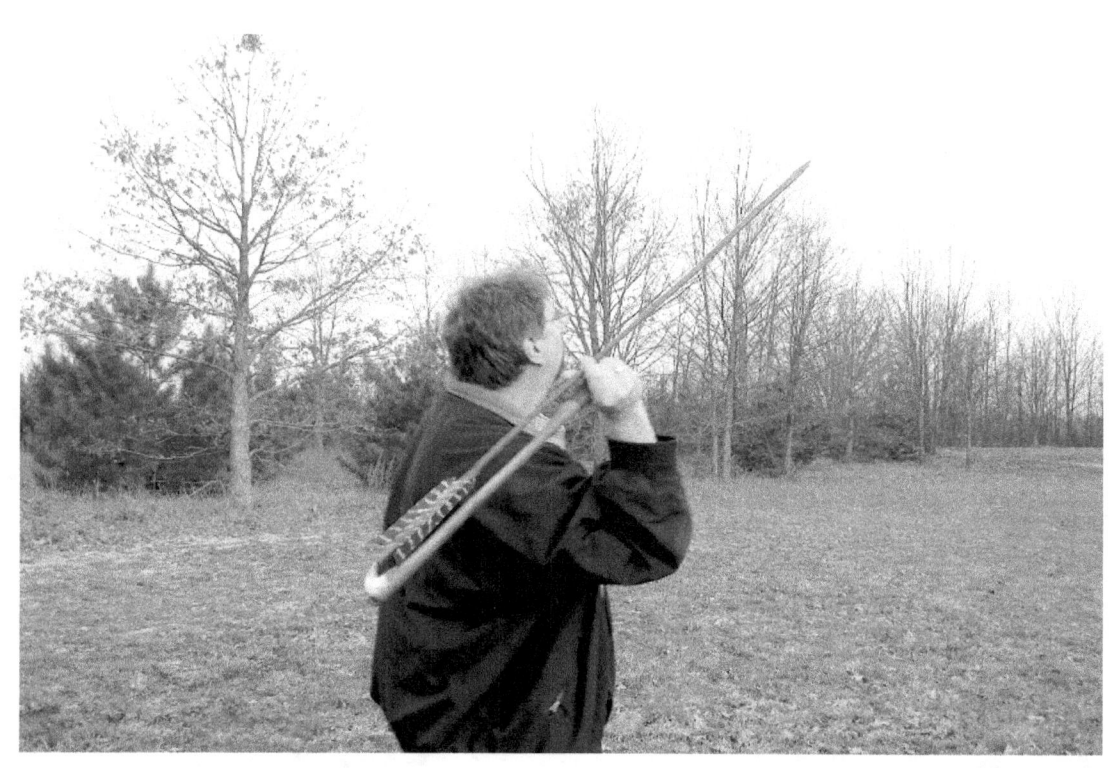

CONVERSIONS

1/4 INCH = .635 cm	4 INCHES = 10.16 cm
3/8 INCH = .952 cm	6 INCHES = 15.24 cm
1/2 INCH = 1.27 cm	36 INCHES = 91.44 cm
1-1/4 INCHES = 3.75 cm	48 INCHES = 121.92 cm
2 INCHES = 5.08 cm	60 INCHES = 152.4 cm
3 INCHES = 7.62 cm	

THE TOMATO STAKE DART

The Tomato Stake Dart is good looking, inexpensive, and quick to make from readily available materials, making it an ideal dart project for the beginner. It's also great for anyone on a budget. I was able to find a bundle of twelve tomato stakes for five dollars. The threaded rod ran around two dollars. The feathers were from a turkey hunt and I had glue and sinew on hand, so my cost for a dozen darts was around eight dollars. That's less than a dollar a dart!

These darts are fletched very much the same way "Ötzi the Iceman" fletched his arrows about 5,000 years ago. The ballast of this dart doubles as the tip. The length can be adjusted to tune the flight characteristics of the dart. (See Appendix for more information on how weight and spine affect dart flight.)

Although this dart is slightly shorter and a bit stiffer than most designs, if care is taken in its manufacture it will perform rather well. Basic dart-making techniques and principles used here will be built upon in the more advanced dart designs that follow.

PARTS

BAMBOO TOMATO STAKE

Look for these at your local garden center. They are a seasonal item so stock up when they're available, unless you wish to purchase them through the internet. Lengths vary, but the ones I've used measure approximately 60" long and I wouldn't go any shorter than that. Bamboo tomato stakes can be found in various colors. I've seen natural, brown stained and green painted stakes.

THREADED STEEL ROD

We'll use a 3/8 inch diameter rod, available in 36 and 48 inch lengths at your local hardware or building supply store.

TURKEY FEATHERS

Choose natural barred or white full length turkey feathers. (See the Materials Source List in the Appendix for suppliers.)

SINEW

Artificial or real sinew may be used. (If you use real sinew please refer to the Appendix for more information about sinew and how to use it.)

EPOXY

Five-minute epoxy was used for this project. If you choose another type of epoxy, you will need to adjust drying times accordingly.

ASSEMBLY

STEP ONE: STRAIGHTEN THE TOMATO STAKE

Because tomato stakes are normally quite crooked, you'll need to straighten them. We'll use heat to do that, which is the way American Indians did it for thousands of years. Our heat source is a live flame such as that from a camp stove. Keep the stake twirling steadily above the flame so you don't scorch, weaken or break it. Heat the joints and sections that need to be straightened one at a time until they begin to sweat. Bend the stake into the desired shape, holding it until it cools. It doesn't have to be perfectly straight, but get it as close as you can.

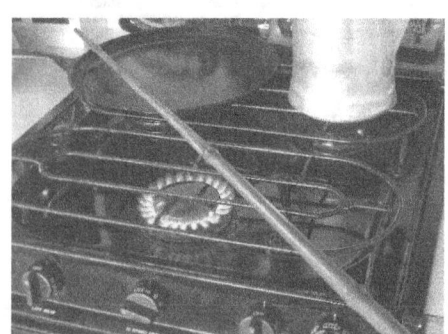

Left: *Heating the cane*

Right: *Straightening the cane*

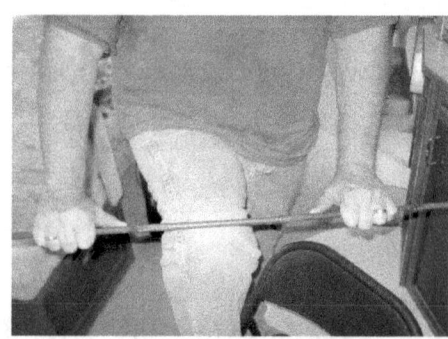

STEP TWO: ADDING THE BALLAST WEIGHT/TIP

Using a hack saw, cut a 3 inch piece off the threaded rod. This will be used as the ballast and tip for the dart. Using a 3/8 inch bit, drill a hole into the large diameter end of the tomato stake. (Because each bamboo stake is unique, it may not be necessary to drill out the end. It will depend on where the nodes are located and how big the opening is.) Mix up the epoxy according to the directions on the 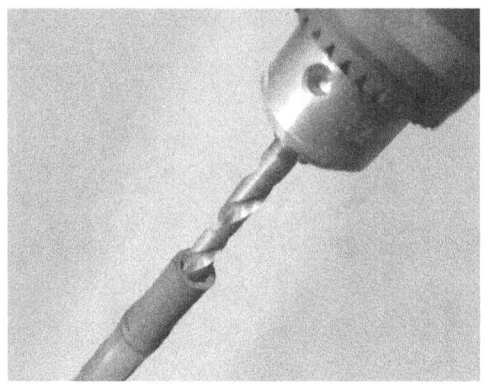 package and apply it to 2 inches of the threaded rod, leaving 1 inch free of glue.

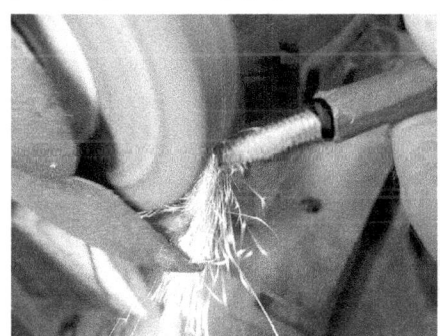 Insert the threaded rod into the large end of the stake to a depth of 2 inches, twisting slowly as the rod is inserted. Place the bamboo stake on its side so the rod will not slide down further into the shaft, and let dry.

After the glue is completely set and dry, grind or file the tip end of the threaded rod to a point.

STEP THREE: FLETCHING THE DART

This will be a two-fletch dart. The fletching goes on the smaller diameter end of the stake. You may need to cut off just a bit of the small end of the dart to make sure it's sturdy enough to make a strong "nock" end for the dart.

To make the fletching you'll need to take your full length feather and split it in half lengthwise down the center of the quill in order to give you two separate feather halves. Start by using a pair of scissors to halve the thicker base end of the feather. When you get to the thinner part of the feather you may find it easier to switch to a craft or utility knife. Use sandpaper to flatten and smooth the bottom of the quill.

Cut the feathers to a length of six inches. Apply a dot of either epoxy, hide glue, or Duco® cement to the back and front ends of a fletching feather.

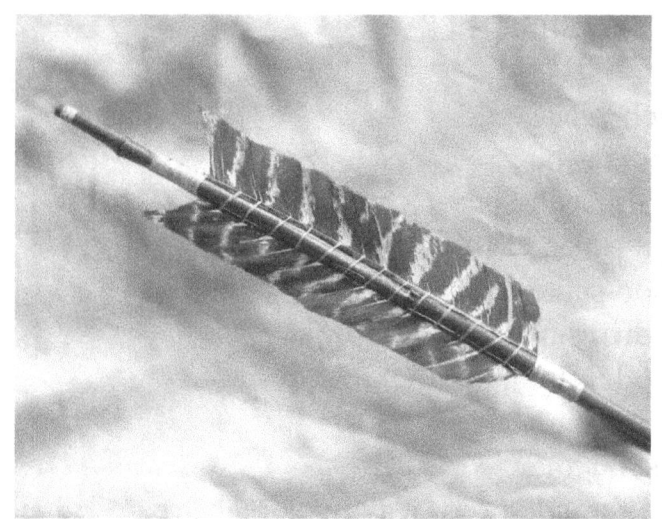

Position the feather on the shaft so the back of the fletching is about 3 inches from the socket end of the dart. Hold it in place with straight pins. Repeat with the other feather, placing it exactly opposite the previous one.

After the glue has dried, apply wraps to the back end of the fletching, wrapping right over the feathers for about ½ to ¾ inch. Tie off the wraps. (See the Appendix for using and tying off sinew.) Next, apply wraps to the front end of the feathers.

After you have tied off the wrapping at the front, apply one more wrap to the fletching by starting at the back and making several wraps over your previous ones. Continue on, making snug evenly spaced wraps that go right down through the feathers to the bottom. The wrap will end up in a nice spiral down the shaft. When you reach the end, apply a few more wraps and tie off the end of the sinew.

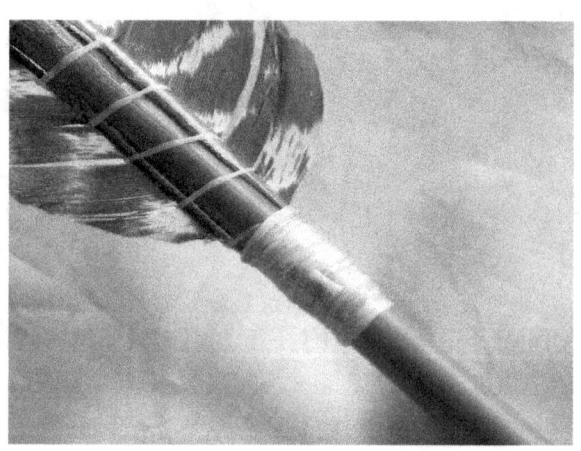

Trim the feathers to a height of about 1¼ to 2 inches. You can trim off the excess feather material that sticks out from under the wraps if you wish, or leave it in place.

STEP FOUR: DRILL THE SOCKET IN THE BASE

Use a ¼ inch diameter bit to drill the hollowed out part into the fletched end of the dart to a depth of about ¼ inch. Smooth it out with fine sandpaper. Wrap the base end tightly with sinew wraps in order to reinforce it.

THE PALEO STYLE DART

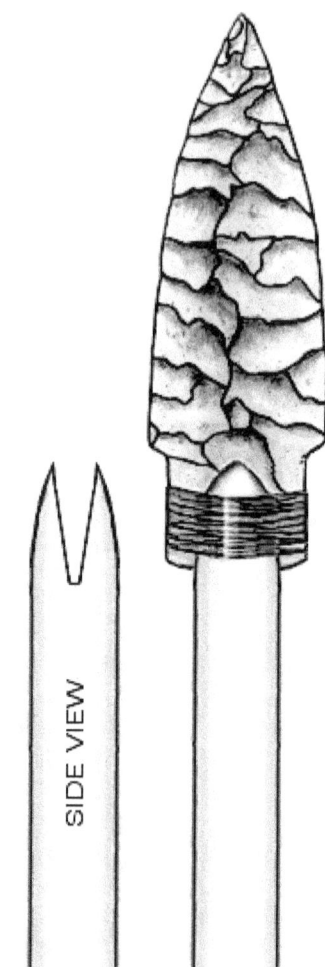

SIDE VIEW

12 TO 14 INCHES

2"

A TWO - FLETCHED DART WITH A VERY NICE PALEO LOOK. FEATHERS ARE ATTACHED TO THE DART IN A STYLE VERY MUCH LIKE THE WAY "ÖTZI THE ICEMAN" FLETCHED HIS ARROWS ABT. 5000 YEARS AGO.

TRY USING WHITE OR BARRED TURKEY FEATHERS OR DARK GOOSE FEATHERS. DIRECTIONS ARE GIVEN IN THIS SECTION FOR HOW TO MAKE FLETCHING FROM WHOLE FEATHERS.

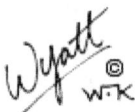

THE DART FORESHAFT IS ABOUT 12 TO 14 INCHES LONG. THE END CAN BE SHARPENED AND FIRE HARDENED AS DESCRIBED IN THE INSTRUCTIONS, OR YOU MAY WISH TO MODIFY IT TO ACCEPT A TRADITIONALLY HAFTED STONE POINT AS SHOWN ABOVE. AFTER PREPARING THE SHAFT, USE HAFTING GLUE MADE FROM PITCH TO AFFIX THE POINT TO THE TIP. AFTER THE GLUE COOLS, APPLY SINEW WRAPS TO FURTHER SECURE THE POINT. (SEE PGS. 82-83 FOR MORE INFORMATION ON HAFTING WITH PITCH AND SINEW.)

HERE'S A RECIPE FOR HAFTING GLUE:

5 PARTS PINE PITCH, 1 PART CHARCOAL (GROUND TO A POWDER), 1 PART BEESWAX (OR TALLOW)

MELT THE PITCH. DO NOT ALLOW IT TO BOIL. THOROUGHLY MIX IN THE CHARCOAL AND BEESWAX. TO MAKE PITCH STICKS, GATHER THE PITCH MIXTURE INTO 3/4" DIAMETER BALLS ONTO THE ENDS OF STICKS AND ALLOW THEM TO COOL.

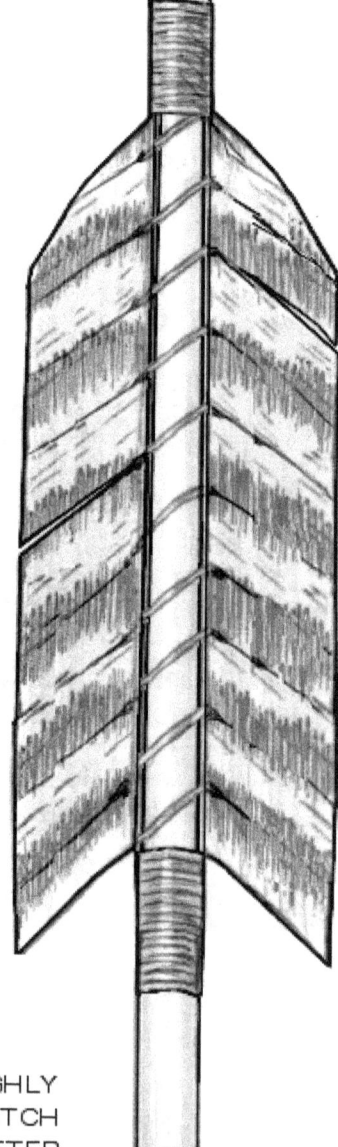

THE PALEO STYLE DART

This is a cane dart much like the ones that may have been used 12,000 years ago by prehistoric Indians in North America. It has a hardwood foreshaft and is fletched with two feathers. There is also an option for adding a traditionally hafted point. This dart looks authentic and, providing care is taken in its construction, it performs very well. There are many people around the world hunting and competing with river cane darts.

In ancient times the foreshaft was often made so that it came out of the dart after it penetrated the animal. A hunter could have a quiver of these stone tipped foreshafts and after recovering the body of the dart he could "reload" it and fire again.

PARTS

RIVER CANE

River cane is the American version of bamboo. For this project you'll need a piece long enough to make the finished dart shaft length 66 inches long (167.64 cm) after trimming, so you'll want to start with a longer piece. The large end needs to be ½ inch (1.27 cm) in diameter. Don't worry if the cane is crooked, you'll be straightening it later.

In a pinch, you can substitute a bamboo tomato stake, but be aware that if you do, you may need to make some adjustments in order to make sure the finished dart is properly tuned. For example, the foreshaft may need to be lengthened. (See Appendix for Dart Making And Usage Tips.)

33

TURKEY FEATHERS

Choose natural barred or white full length turkey feathers.

FORESHAFT

You'll need a ½ inch (1.27 cm) diameter hardwood dowel that is 12 to 14 inches in length (30.48 to 35.56 cm). Or, if you're up for the challenge, you can find a nice straight branch cut from a suitable hardwood tree and shape it to the above dimensions.

SINEW

Artificial or real sinew may be used. (If you use real sinew please refer to the Appendix for more information about sinew and how to use it.)

ASSEMBLY

STEP ONE: STRAIGHTEN THE CANE SHAFT

Trim the small end of the cane to make it more sturdy, while allowing for a shaft length of 66 inches.

You'll need to straighten the river cane, as we did with the Tomato Stake Dart, using a live flame such as the burner of a camp stove. Keep the cane twirling steadily above the flame (not directly in the flame) so you don't scorch, weaken or break it. Heat the joints and sections that need to be straightened one at a time until they begin to sweat. Bend the cane into the desired shape, holding it until it cools. It doesn't need to be perfectly straight--get it as close as you can.

STEP TWO: FLETCHING THE DART

This will be a two-fletch dart, employing the same method used for the Tomato Stake Dart. The fletching goes on the smaller diameter end of the cane.

To make the fletching you'll need to take your full length feather and split it in half lengthwise down the center of the quill in order to give you two separate feather halves. Start by using a pair of scissors to halve the thicker base end of the feather. When you get to the thinner part of the feather you may find it easier to switch to a craft or utility knife. Use sandpaper to flatten and smooth the bottom of the quill.

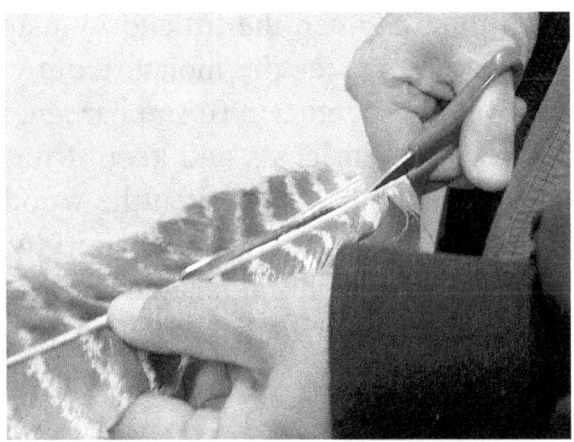

Cut the feathers to a length of 6 inches. Although "Ötzi" used birch pitch, we're going to apply a dot of either epoxy, hide glue, or Duco® cement to the back and front ends of a feather. Position the feather on the shaft so the back of the fletching is about 3 to 4 inches (7.62 to 10.16 cm) from the socket end of the dart. Hold it in place with straight pins. Repeat with the other feather, placing it exactly opposite the previous one.

After the glue has dried, apply wraps to the back end of the fletching, wrapping right over the feathers for about ½ inch (1.27 cm). Tie off the wraps. (See the Appendix for using and tying off sinew.) Next, apply wraps to the front end of the feathers. After you have tied off the wrapping at the front, apply one more wrap to the fletching by starting at the back and making several wraps over your previous ones. Continue on, making snug evenly spaced wraps that go right down through the feathers to the bottom. The wrap will end up in a nice spiral down the shaft as shown in the drawing on Page 32. When you reach the end, apply a few more wraps and tie off the end of the sinew.

Trim the feathers to a height of 1¼ to 2 inches (3.75 to 5.08 cm). You can trim off the excess feather material that sticks out from under the wraps, if you wish, or leave it in place. It has been done both ways historically.

STEP THREE: SHAPING AND PREPARING THE FORESHAFT

Sharpen one end of the foreshaft to a point as shown in the drawing. If you are using the wood from a hardwood branch to make your foreshaft, you may wish to strengthen the tip end by using the ancient technique of fire hardening. This process takes the moisture out of the wood and as a result the fibers shrink very tightly together. To fire harden, hold the tip end of the foreshaft a few inches above some hot coals and keep it turning constantly. Do not let it get burned or scalded, as that will weaken the wood. The drying process can take a little while so just be very patient and keep it twirling over the flame. When the wood gets a very "matte" or dull appearance you are finished. Whether you use a hardwood dowel or a hardwood branch to make the foreshaft, you may want to end by burnishing the point end with a piece of smooth bone to further compress the fibers.

When the tip end is finished, the diameter on the other end of the foreshaft is then filed down for a length of about 2 inches (5.08 cm) so that it will fit snugly into the end of the main shaft. Leave a nice shoulder on it so it won't get pushed further into the dart and cause the shaft to split. (Refer to drawing on Page 32.)

STEP FOUR: ATTACHING THE FORESHAFT TO THE DART

Prepare the end of the main shaft to receive the foreshaft by drilling a 3/8" (.952 cm) hole in it to a depth of two inches (5.08 cm). If you wish, you can use epoxy to glue the foreshaft into the larger diameter end of the cane dart shaft. Wrap the end of the cane shaft securely with a continuous wrap of sinew for a distance of 2 inches (5.08 cm) which will provide reinforcement for the joint.

STEP FIVE: DRILL THE SOCKET IN THE BASE

Use a ¼ inch (.635 cm) diameter bit to drill the hollowed out part into the fletched end of the dart to a depth of about ¼ inch. Smooth it out with fine sandpaper. Wrap the base end tightly with sinew wraps in order to reinforce it.

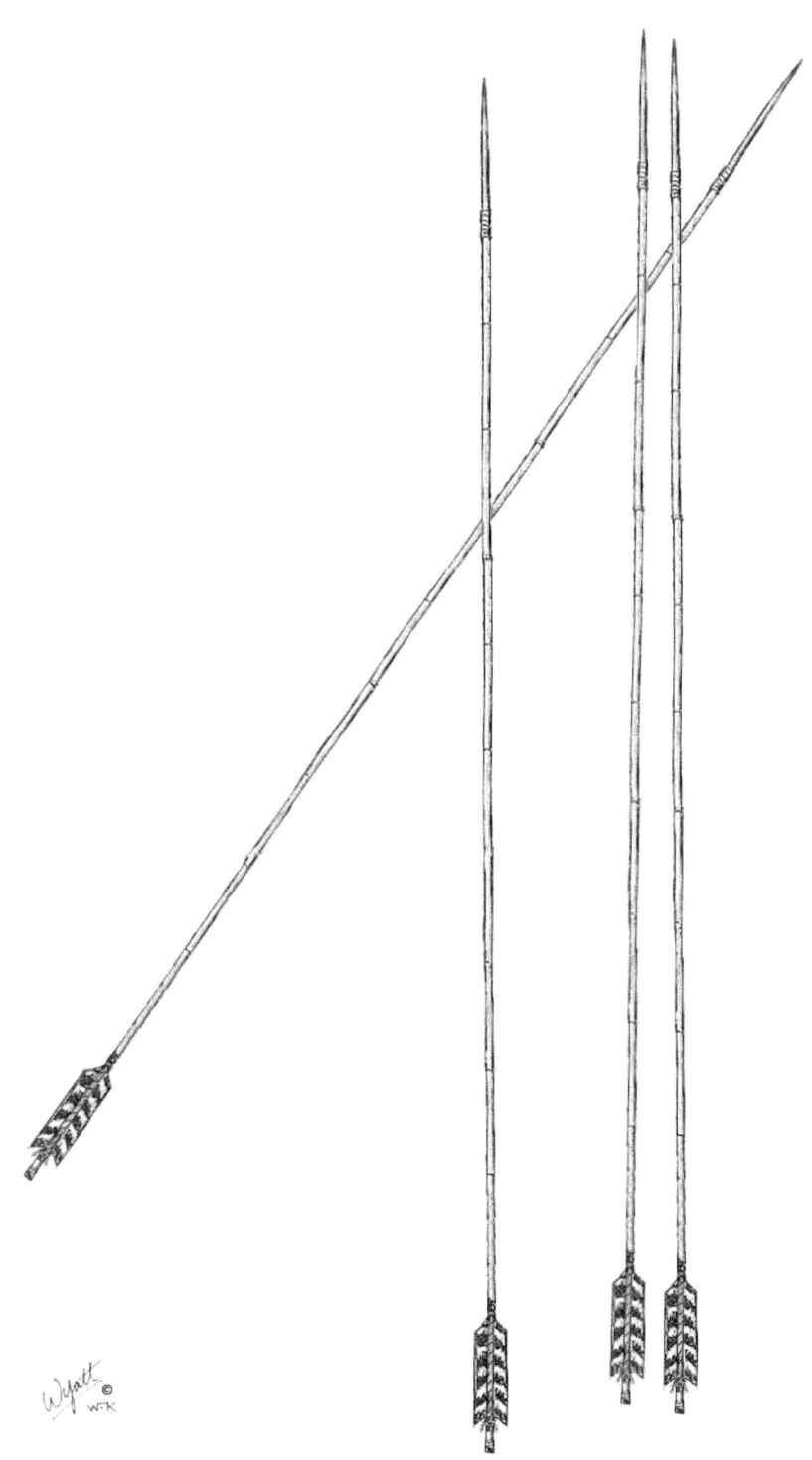

CARBON FIBER
CONTEMPORARY DART

This excellent dart has been used with great success in competition, hunting and fishing. It is extremely accurate. The tip end of this highly versatile dart will accept several different styles of points or broadheads which can be screwed on as needed. (See Page 45 for a "take-down" variation of this dart.)

This dart was designed by Michigan atlatlist Chris Oberg after hearing about a friend's experience with Gold Tip® arrow shafting material. This durable dart has internal weight adjustments for balance and is easily produced with a minimum of tools or expertise. Because this dart uses arrow shafting it won't damage 3-D targets and is widely accepted at archery ranges.

Here's a summary of what we'll be doing: We'll take a motor mount that's been reduced in size to fit inside the arrow shafts and glue it in as a connector for the two shafts, making a permanent one-piece dart.

PARTS

2 GOLD TIP® (HUNTER) 75-95 CARBON ARROW SHAFTS

Comprised of 5 cross-laminated layers of carbon fiber wrap, these shafts are so strong that conventional point inserts can be used without danger of splitting the thin-walled carbon tube. Outside tube diameter is 5/16 inch, inside diameter is .245 inches. The shaft length is 32.5 inches. The 75-95 tube is recommended because it allows greater weight behind the tip without over-flexing during the power stroke of the throw. Two of these shafts will be glued together to make one dart.

MOTOR MOUNT STUD

You'll need a ¼ inch diameter hardened 2-inch long motor mount stud from your local automotive supply store.

JB WELD®

This is a very strong cold-weld compound, so strong it is used as an alternative to welding. It comes in two parts that need to be mixed together as you would most epoxies.

1/4 INCH THREADED ROD - 3 TO 5 INCHES LONG

2 FEMALE POINT INSERTS

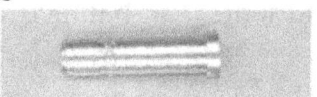

1 SCREW-ON 145-GRAIN FIELD POINT (5/16" DIAMETER)

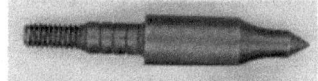

3 FULL CUT PRE-GROUND FLETCHING FEATHERS

You will also need WHITE FLETCH-LAC®, FLETCH-TITE® and ACETONE.

ASSEMBLY

STEP ONE: JOINING THE ARROW SHAFTS

Prepare the tubes by gently abrading the inside with 100-grit sandpaper. Use a cotton swab with acetone. The threads on each end of the motor mount are filed down slightly to remove any sharp edges that would damage the inside of the tube as the dart flexes.

Before gluing, test fit the motor mount. The center non-threaded section may need to be reduced slightly so it fits into the arrow shaft. This can be done by chucking it up in an electric hand drill and removing enough material with a mill file to make it fit. Once you are satisfied with how the motor mount fits into the arrow shaft, degrease it with acetone.

Mix up some JB Weld® according to the instructions and apply it to the motor mount, cementing it in place between the two carbon tubes. (A more durable bond can be achieved by the following: Before applying the glue, take a ¼ inch threading tap and screw it a short distance into each arrow shaft and then remove it in order to score the inside of the arrow shaft. Tests have shown there is very little chance of separation or loose joints after this type of scoring is done.) Don't worry about adding any additional support to the tubes, the Gold Tip® carbon shaft has enough inherent strength. Set assembly aside for 24 hours to dry.

MOTOR MOUNT JOINT

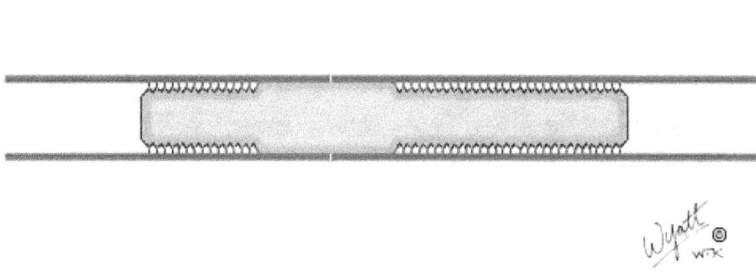

STEP TWO - ADDING BALLAST AND ASSEMBLING TIP END

For this project the weight provided by a 5-inch length of threaded rod is used. You may want to experiment with different lengths in order to influence the dart weight. Before making your decision, I recommend consulting the Appendix where you will find further information on how ballast weight affects darts.

Lightly sand the inside of one end of the dart shaft and clean it with acetone on a cotton swab. Apply JB Weld® to the entire surface of the threaded rod and insert it into the shaft. Immediately apply JB Weld® to a female point insert. Push it into the end until the shoulder is flush with the end of the shaft, setting the placement of the ballast in the process. Put the dart aside to dry for 24 hours, making sure the tip end is down to prevent the rod from shifting.

TIP END WITH BALLAST

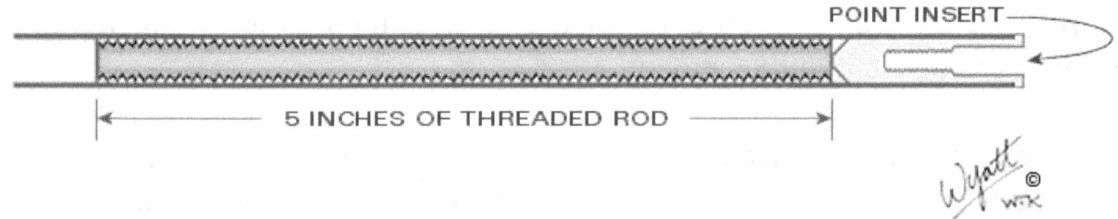

STEP THREE - FLETCHING AND FINISHING THE DART

The fletching is applied in 120 degree increments around the shaft. Either pre-ground shaped feathers or plastic vanes can be used. A Bitzenburger fletching jig is very helpful in this process. To use one for this project, make a temporary nock from a short section of ¼ inch threaded rod which will be used to index in the Bitzenburger. Degrease the dart shaft opposite the ballast end with acetone, and dip the area to be fletched in white Fletch-Lac®. Set up the Bitzenburger for a straight fletch. After lightly sanding the base, apply Fletch-Tite® glue to the vane and hold it in place against the shaft. Let dry. Repeat with remaining two feathers, taking care to index 120 degrees for each one.

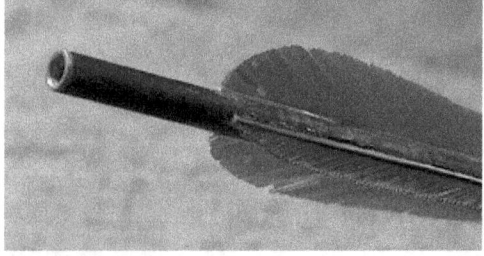

The fletched end of the dart with the female point insert epoxied in place -- a nice way to finish off the end of the dart and to provide reinforcement and protection from wear.

When all the fletching has dried, degrease the inside of the open end of the shaft. Use JB Weld® to glue a point insert into the end. This will serve as a thrower hook receiver. When the weld is dry your dart is finished!

I've been very happy with this dart style and have had many people admire it and comment on its clean professional appearance and on its consistently good performance. This dart is ideal for competition, as well as hunting and fishing applications. Its versatile design allows for the use of all kinds of "screw-in" broadheads, tips, fishing points, etc. With a good atlatl and a handful of these darts, one has all the makings for a fun time at the range or hunting out in the field.

*Six time Michigan Atlatl State Champion **Chris Oberg** first became interested in the atlatl after attending a "mastodon barbecue picnic" back in 1996. His background in graphic art came in handy as he reproduced historically accurate museum replica throwing sticks based on dimensions, descriptions and images found in scientific articles. Chris was able to share much of his research and his discoveries about atlatl and dart form and function in the Michigan Atlatl Association Newsletter during his tenure as its editor.*

Chris' training techniques as former head fencing coach at MSU, along with his experience in atlatl competitions, have taught him that frequent practice emphasizing form, balance and angular momentum using well-balanced correctly spined darts, results in repeatable dart accuracy and good scores.

CONVERSIONS

.245 INCH	=	.622 cm
1/4 INCH	=	.635 cm
5/16 INCH	=	.793 cm
2 INCHES	=	5.08 cm
3 INCHES	=	7.62 cm
5 INCHES	=	12.7 cm
32.5 INCHES	=	82.55 cm

"TAKE-DOWN" CARBON FIBER CONTEMPORARY DART

This "take-down" dart was also designed by Chris Oberg and is a variation of the one-piece Carbon Fiber Dart previously described. While it retains all of the excellent features of the one-piece Carbon Fiber Dart, it has the added advantage of breaking down into two sections, making it much more convenient to handle and transport. I carry my "take-down" darts, along with an atlatl or two, in an arrow quiver.

This is my favorite contemporary dart. Aside from its portability and smart design, I like the fact that the dart has the same diameter as an arrow. Unlike darts made of traditional materials, I can throw these carbon fiber darts at archery ranges without tearing up the targets.

PARTS

2 GOLD TIP® (HUNTER) 75 - 95 CARBON ARROW SHAFTS

Comprised of 5 cross-laminated layers of carbon fiber wrap, these shafts are so strong that conventional point inserts can be used without danger of splitting the thin-walled carbon tube. Outside tube diameter is 5/16 inch, inside diameter is .245 inches. The shaft length is 32.5 inches. The 75-95 tube is recommended because it allows greater weight behind the tip without over-flexing during the power stroke of the throw. Two shafts will be needed to make one dart.

JB WELD®

This is a very strong epoxy that's used as an alternative to welding in some applications. It comes in two parts that need to be mixed together.

1/4 INCH THREADED ROD - 3 TO 5 INCHES LONG

1 SCREW-ON 145-GRAIN FIELD POINT (5/16 INCH DIAMETER)

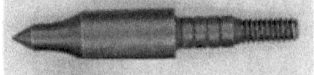

3 FULL CUT PRE-GROUND FLETCHING FEATHERS

3 FEMALE POINT INSERTS

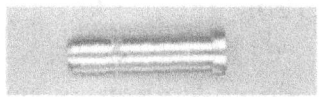

You will also need WHITE FLETCH-LAC®, FLETCH-TITE® and ACETONE.

ASSEMBLY

STEP ONE: JOINING THE ARROW SHAFTS

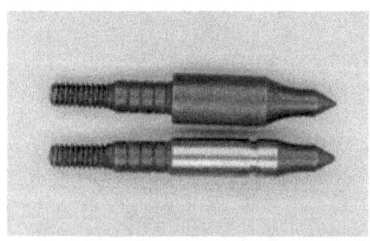

Above: *Two field points. The bottom one shows how the field point should look after being reduced in diameter.*

Below: *Two female point inserts. The one on the bottom shows how the insert should look after the lip is reduced in diameter.*

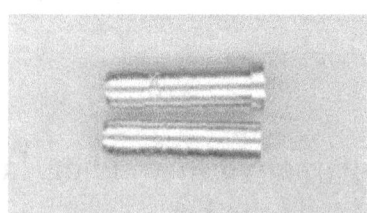

Reduce the diameter of the 145 grain field point to .245 inches so that it can slip into an arrow shaft. This job is best done on a lathe, but in a pinch you can chuck the field point into an electric drill and reduce its diameter with a flat file. A groove can be added to the field point to accept cement for a stronger bond. Set aside for later use.

Take the female point insert and remove the lip or reduce it to .245 inches in diameter.   This will enable it to be inserted into one end of an arrow shaft. The female point insert will need to be glued into the end of the shaft exactly ¼ inch below flush. A consistent ¼ inch depth will allow for the interchange of components in the event you make more darts. If you damage the front or back half of your dart you can screw in a replacement shaft that fits just like the original. Below you will find a drawing showing how to make a simple gauge for insuring consistent depth for the placement and gluing of the female point insert.

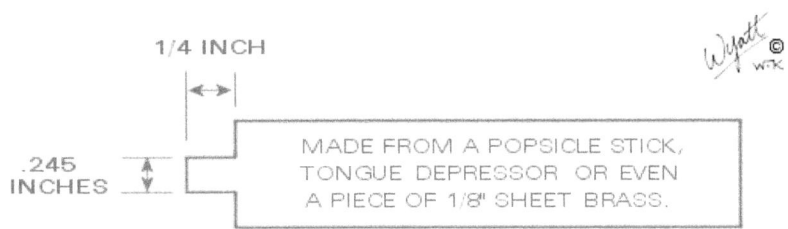

1/4 INCH DEPTH GAUGE

1/4 INCH

.245 INCHES

MADE FROM A POPSICLE STICK, TONGUE DEPRESSOR OR EVEN A PIECE OF 1/8" SHEET BRASS.

Now you are ready to glue the female point insert into the shaft. Lightly sand the inside of the tube and clean it with acetone on a cotton swab. Mix up pea-sized blobs of parts A and B of the JB Weld® and smear some on the outside of the reduced female point insert but first plug the hole in the bottom of the female insert so epoxy will not migrate or get on the female insert threads. Use a toothpick to apply the remainder of the JB Weld® to the inside of the arrow shaft.

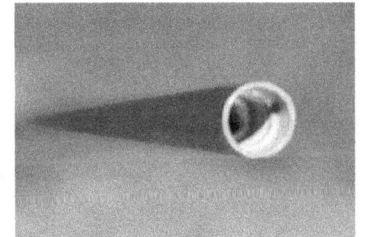

A look at the finished end of the first arrow shaft showing how the modified female point insert sits ¼ inch below flush inside the tube.

Insert the female reduced point insert into the arrow shaft using the .245 inch end of the depth gauge you made to seat the female insert exactly ¼ inch below flush. CAREFULLY wipe up any exposed epoxy on the inside lip of the arrow shaft with acetone on a cotton swab. *Don't bump or move the female reduced point insert.* Lay this "female arrow shaft assembly" aside horizontally so the epoxy can cure undisturbed for 24 hours.

Bonding The Take-Down Joint

After the female shaft assembly has dried completely, you can make the "male shaft assembly". Take the other arrow shaft and lightly sand the inner wall of one end and swab it with acetone. Next, run a ¼ inch threaded tap a short distance up the prepared shaft end in order to make a stronger bond.

Take the female shaft assembly and swab the inside of the female point insert with petroleum jelly. (This will allow the screwed-in field point to be removed even if a little epoxy slips in when the two shafts are joined together.) Screw the reduced male field point all the way into the reduced female insert shaft assembly. Do not let any petroleum jelly get onto the exposed part of the reduced field point.

Smear JB Weld® inside the prepared tube. Also, smear JB Weld® on the exposed portion of the field tip that is sticking out of the female shaft assembly. Join the two shafts snugly together. As the glue cures it is very important for the shafts to remain straight. In order to insure this, they should be taped to a board for 24 hours and placed standing up in a corner. Be sure to have the freshly glued joint on top so any excess glue flows onto the tip of the field point.

TAKE-DOWN JOINT

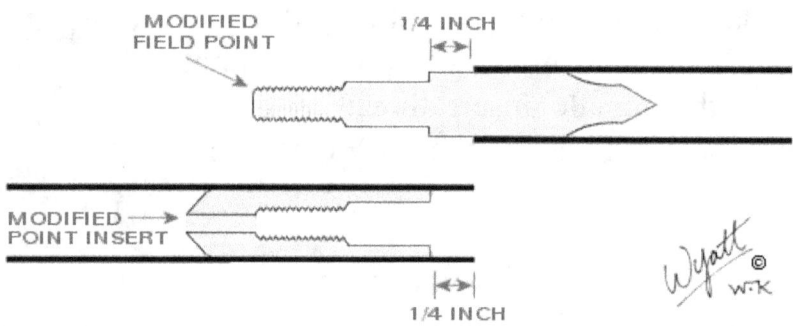

STEP TWO: ADDING BALLAST AND ASSEMBLING TIP END

For this project the weight provided by a 5-inch length of threaded rod is used. You may want to experiment with different lengths in order to influence the dart weight. Before making your decision, I recommend consulting the Appendix where you will find further information on how ballast weight affects darts.

Lightly sand the inside of the open end of the female shaft assembly and clean it with acetone on a cotton swab. Apply JB Weld® to the entire surface of the threaded rod and insert it into the shaft. Immediately apply JB Weld® to the female point insert. Push it into the end until the shoulder is flush with the end of the shaft, setting the placement of the ballast in the process. Put the female shaft assembly aside to dry for 24 hours, making sure the tip end is down to prevent the rod from shifting. After it has dried, you can thread a field point of your choice into the tip end of the dart.

TIP END WITH BALLAST

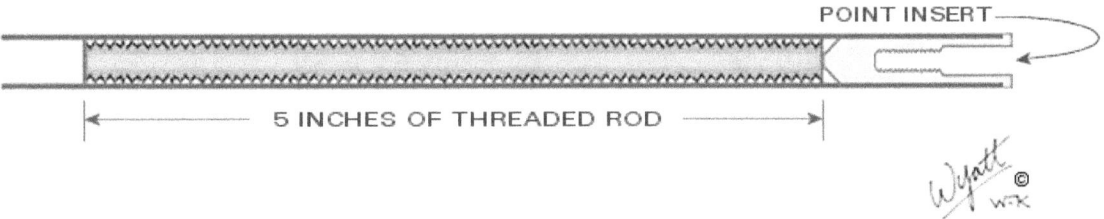

Now screw the two finished shafts together, making one long atlatl dart.

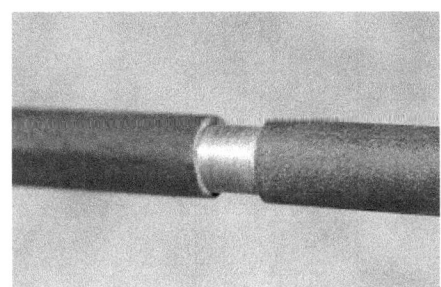

Left: A view of the two shafts being joined together. The shoulder of the male insert has ¼ inch of travel to make into the other tube.

Right: The joint after being screwed together making for a very strong, clean joint for the dart.

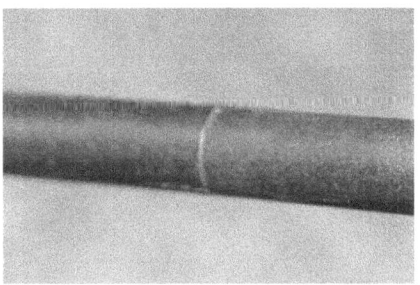

STEP THREE: FLETCHING AND FINISHING THE DART

The fletching will be applied in 120 degree increments around the male shaft assembly on the end opposite the joint. Either pre-ground shaped feathers or plastic vanes can be used. A Bitzenburger fletching jig is very helpful in this process. To use one for this project, make a temporary nock from a short section of ¼ inch threaded rod which will be used to index in the Bitzenburger. Degrease the area to be fletched with acetone, and then dip it in white Fletch-Lac®. Set up the Bitzenburger for a straight fletch. After lightly sanding the area, apply

Fletch-Tite® glue to the vane and hold it in place against the shaft. Let dry. Repeat with remaining two feathers, taking care to index 120 degrees for each one.

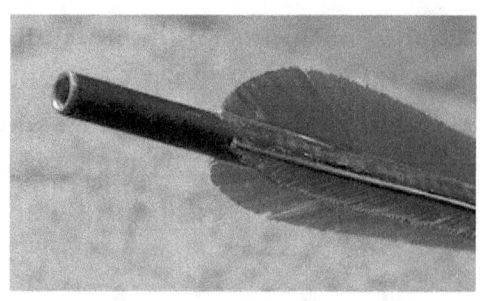

When all the fletching has dried, degrease the inside of the open end of the shaft. Use JB Weld® to glue a point insert into the fletching end of the shaft. This will serve as a thrower hook receiver.

A look at the fletched end of the dart with the female point insert epoxied in place -- a nice way to finish off the end of the dart and to provide reinforcement and protection from wear.

CONVERSIONS

.245 INCH	=	.622 cm
1/4 INCH	=	.635 cm
5/16 INCH	=	.793 cm
5 INCHES	=	12.7 cm
32.5 INCHES	=	82.55 cm

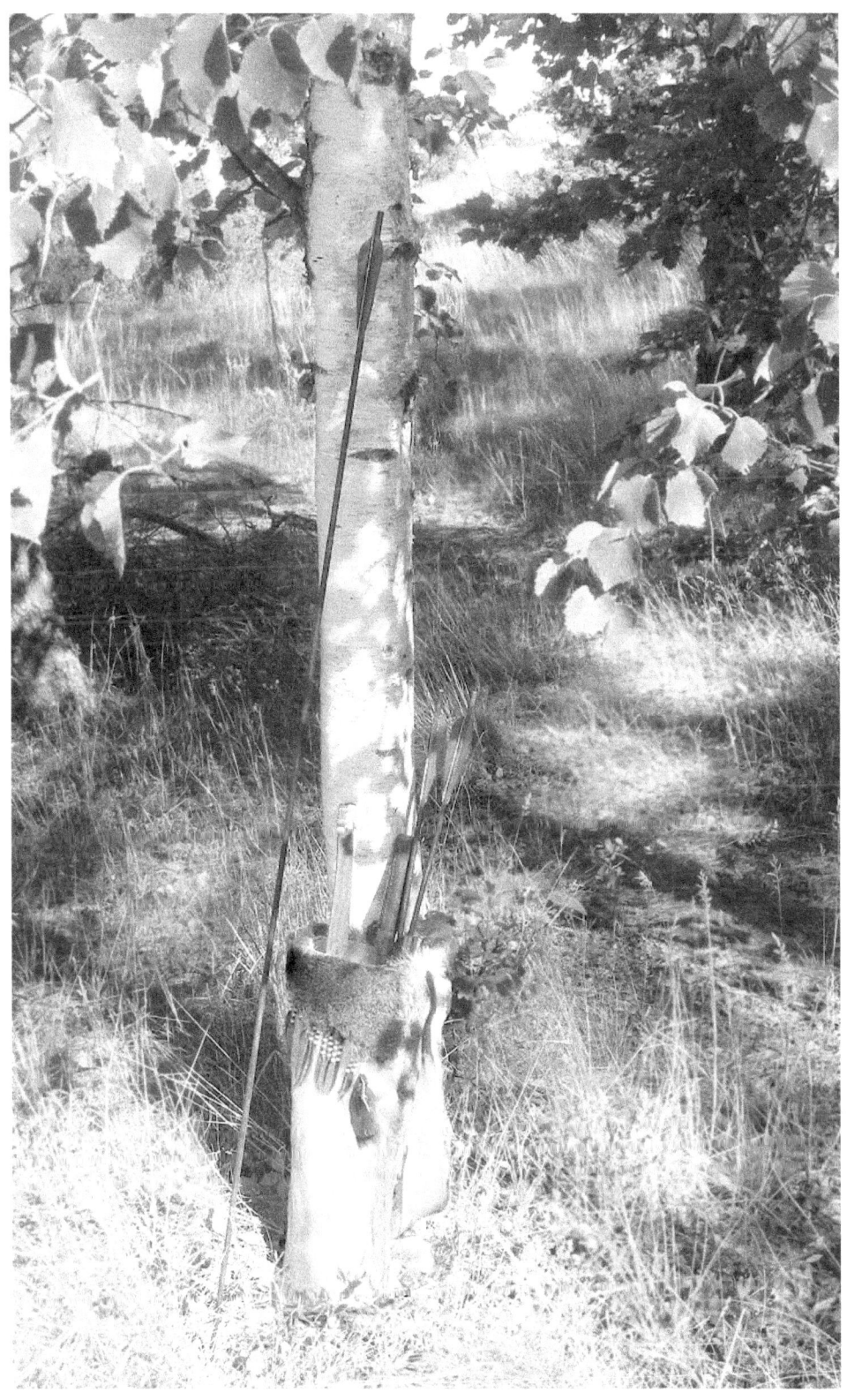

USING THE ATLATL AND DART SYSTEM

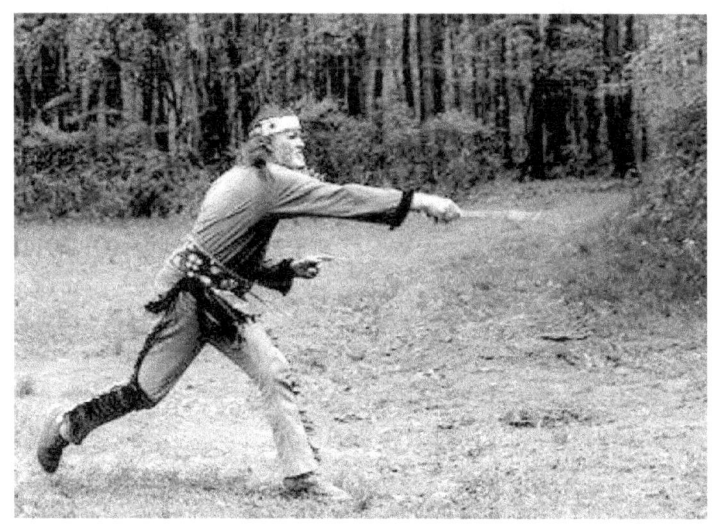

HOW TO USE THE ATLATL

Now that you've built yourself an atlatl and a nice set of darts, it's time to learn how to use them. It won't take long to get the knack of it. But first, let's go over safety one more time.

Always remember the atlatl and dart system is a deadly weapon. Use the same common sense and care you would with a gun or a bow. Be alert and aware of your surroundings. Give yourself plenty of room and remember that wind can effect the flight and path of your dart. Establish a safety line behind the person throwing darts and keep all people and animals well behind it. Do not throw darts if there are people or animals ahead of the safety line. Never allow children to use the atlatl or darts unless they are under close adult supervision. Your adherence to safe conduct will insure a pleasurable experience as you work to improve your skills with this ancient weapon system.

How To Throw Darts With Your Atlatl

For the designs in this book we will use the "hammer style" grip. (See photo on the following page.) Hold the dart lightly with the thumb and forefinger. Stand with your feet apart, left foot forward pointed at the target, the right foot back at a right angle to the left foot. With the dart in place, draw the atlatl

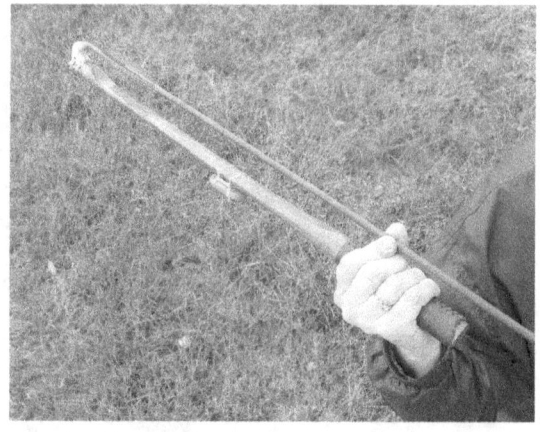

straight back over the shoulder and execute a straight-forward overhand swing as if throwing a paper airplane. (See photos on Page 57.) At the finish of the swing you may find you have rocked forward on the toes of your right foot. Don't try to release the dart with the thumb, it's not necessary. If the thumb is pressed lightly against the dart and not lapped entirely over the top, the release will take place without conscious effort at exactly the right time. Begin with gentle tosses to get the feel of it. As you get more familiar with how the dart behaves, you can gradually increase the distance and power of the cast in order to bring the dart out to the target.

Now it's time to get serious. Find a large outdoor area. Keep the safety rules in mind and you can have a lot of fun seeing just how far you can get your darts to go! For distance you'll need to throw in such a way that the dart follows a higher arc than the flatter trajectories used for target throwing. It's quite satisfying to watch the darts gracefully sail far downfield. Bring someone along and have a friendly competition to see who can throw the farthest. Just for kicks, you may be interested in knowing the current world record distance throw for an atlatl is 848.5 feet (just over 258 meters).

A beginner can practice throwing for accuracy by making a target according to World Atlatl Association's (WAA) International Standards And Accuracy Competition (ISAC) dimensions. Instructions for making one can be found in the Appendix of this workbook. Once made, place your target in front of a dense foam stop or some hay bales and stand 25 feet away. Cast your darts at the bullseye, and after you get the hang of it, move back a few more feet and try again. Continue practicing from these distances, gradually moving back, until you reach 15 meters from the target. Practice 15-meter throws until you feel confident about getting your dart onto the target regularly. Next, move back to 20 meters and do the same thing. Continue regular practice from 15 and 20 meters and you'll soon find yourself hitting the target more and more dependably.

When you feel comfortable with your ability to put your dart into the target, you may want to consider participating in a competition.

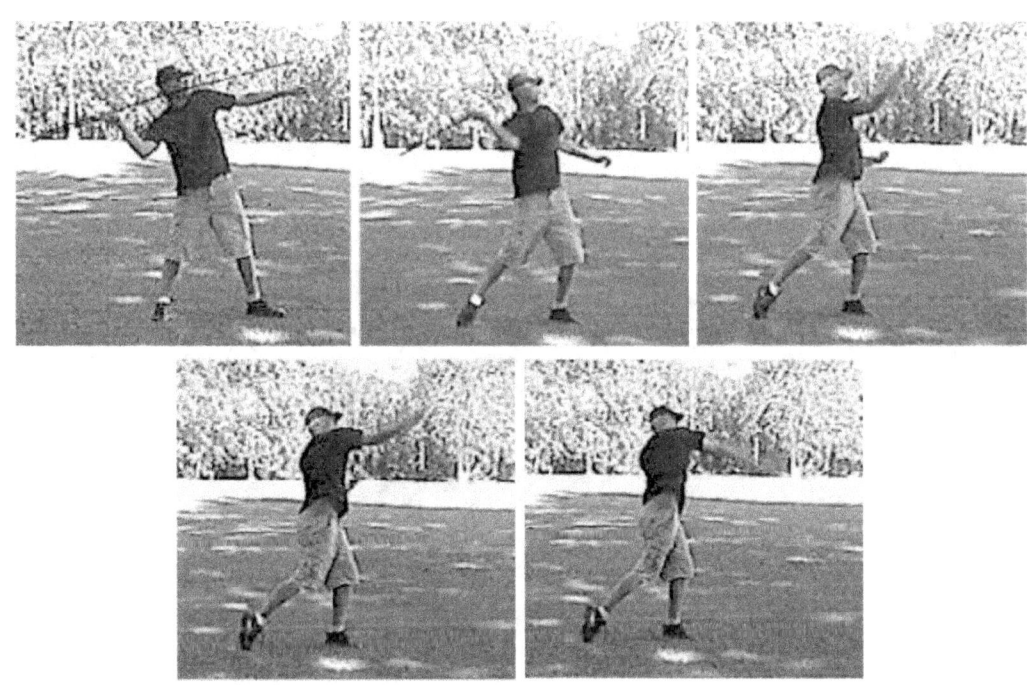

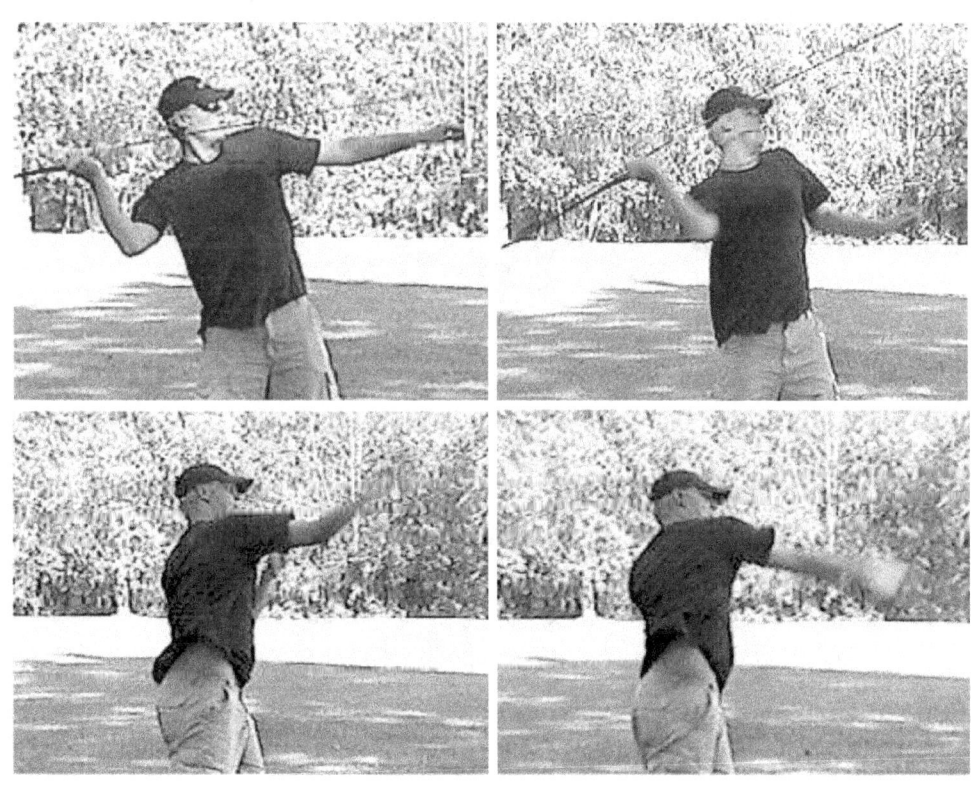

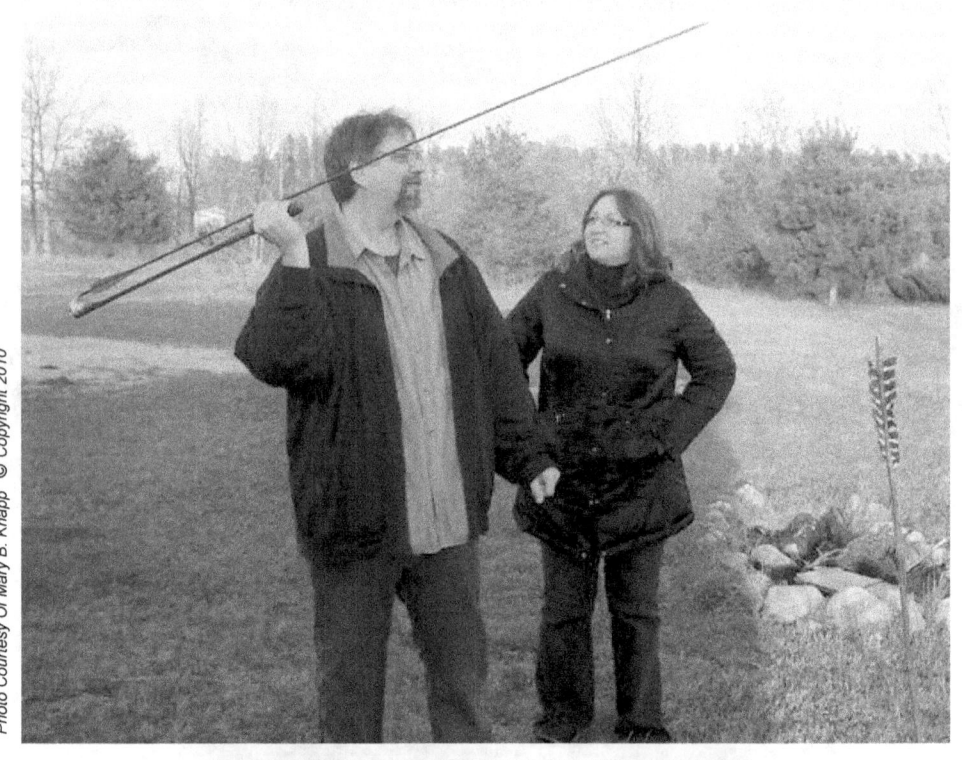

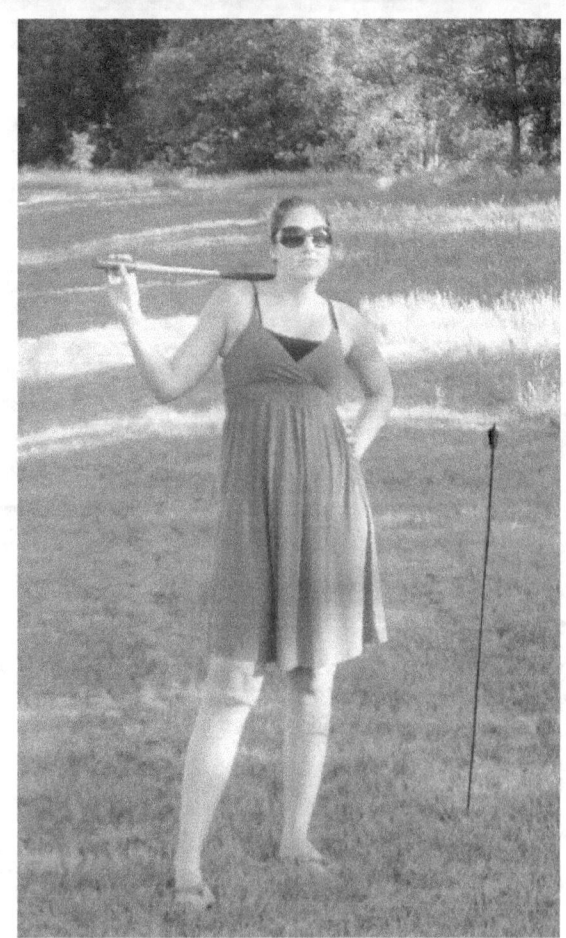

USING THE ATLATL FOR FUN
AND COMPETITION

Below you'll find some games designed to help you develop more skill and accuracy. Have fun, but remember to always keep safety foremost in mind!

Roving Atlatl Darts is played much the same as archery "stump shooting". Two to five players walk through the woods and pick random objects such as soft tree stumps, leaf piles, and other natural targets at which to cast their darts. Whoever gets the most hits is the winner.

Atlatl Golf is particularly enjoyable if you have a large place to play, such as a park or perhaps a golf course late in the year. This game employs nine circles 6 feet in diameter with flags in the center of each, standing about 6 feet above the ground. The flags are to show where the circles are from a distance. Erect 9 tee markers to show the direction to throw for each of the circles. Vary the distance from the tees to the circles from between 50 to 200 yards. Score this game the same as you would in golf. The winner is the person who, after completing the course, has taken the least amount of throws, starting at the tees, to land the point of his dart inside all of the circles. Distances from tee to target of 50 to 75 yards are 2 par, 75 to 180 yards are 3 par and 150 to 200 yards are 4 par.

Atlatl Target Competition. This is a fun one to try with children. The object is to hit a target face about 4 feet in diameter and stapled with wire against a backstop of four to six bales of straw or hay. Try a "kangaroo round" of five throws at a distance of 15 yards from the target, five throws at 20 yards, and five at 25 yards.

Throwing For Distance. Each player will need three darts. Darts should be marked before starting so they can be identified. Each player gets 3 throws per round. For each round the person who throws the farthest dart scores 5 points and the person who throws the tightest grouping of their 3 darts also gets 5 points. The first person to score 50 points is the winner.

Atlatl Competitions

When you feel comfortable with your ability to put your dart into the target, consider participating in a competition. There are various types held around the world. You may find an opportunity to walk an atlatl 3-D course. This is basically a competition where you shoot at animal targets from different distances. Because you are presented with a variety of shooting situations, it's a fun way to challenge your skills.

Many atlatl and dart enthusiasts enjoy competing in accuracy competitions held under the auspices of the WWA (World Atlatl Association) which follow the ISAC (International Standard Accuracy Competition) rules. By using this standard everyone has an opportunity to compete on an equal basis and compare their abilities to others around the world while throwing regionally or locally. This contest identifies the most accurate atlatlist in the world for any given year.

Here's how ISAC competitions work: A target is drawn on a piece of cardboard according to the dimensions indicated in the ISAC rules. In the exact center is a 10 centimeter (about 3.94 inches) circle with an "X" drawn in it. Numbers are placed in the spaces between the circles. If you hit it exactly in the "X" you get a 10X for that throw. If you miss the target or fail to get the dart into any of the rings it is a zero.

You can use either primitive or open (modern materials) equipment. The competitor throws from 15 meters and then 20 meters. A line on the ground indicates where these distances are. If your foot crosses or touches the line when throwing, the cast doesn't count. Each competitor gets 5 throws from each distance. The highest score from the event is the winner. The results of the contest are then mailed to the World Atlatl Association for comparison with all the other events throughout the world.

More detailed information on how the ISAC atlatl competitions work, the rules for competing, and World Atlatl Association contact information is provided on Page 75 in the Appendix of this book. You may want to read it over in order to get familiar with what to expect in competition as you practice throwing.

So consider participating in a competition. You'll find them to be friendly affairs. Keep in mind, every person out there competing remembers what it was like to be a beginner, so don't worry about being "good enough". You'll find plenty of support along the way as you get better and better at your new obsession.

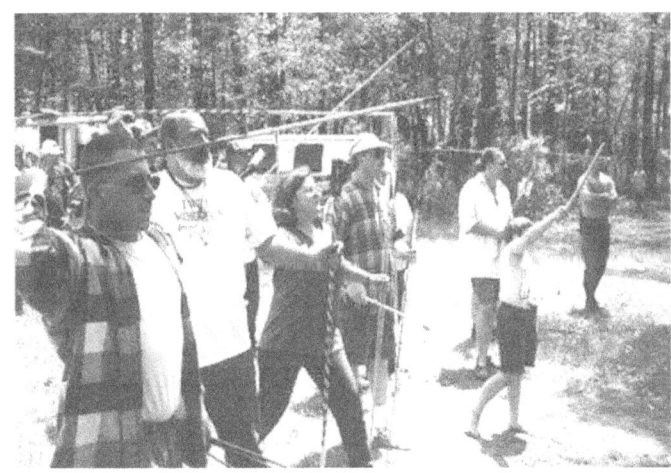

HUNTING AND FISHING WITH THE ATLATL AND DART

It's back! After so many centuries where the atlatl and dart system was forgotten and its secrets lost, here it comes out of the mist of those faraway times to take its place once again in the hands of the modern day hunter.

The atlatl and dart has been used in recent times to take every kind of game the bow and arrow has. It has been effective in harvesting deer, wild boar, African big game animals, small game and more.

Atlatl and dart hunting requires a great amount of understanding about the behavior of the animal being hunted, the environment, and the effective range of the weapon. It demands stealth in tracking and stalking, discipline in preparation, and thousands of hours of practice to assure accurate and effective shot placement. For the hunter who is no longer challenged by the modern methods, or one who wants to connect on a more personal level with the outdoors and the game animal, atlatl hunting is supreme. It represents the ultimate challenge to the modern hunter--the taking of game with an effective stone age weapon.

Preparation

If you are new to atlatl hunting you'll need to be aware of a number of things. You'll want to check out what the local hunting laws are in your area and buy the appropriate licenses. Some states don't allow atlatl hunting yet. Many times it's only available on privately owned preserves.

You should make sure you've practiced enough to become proficient before hunting. You want to dispatch the animal as humanely and quickly as possible. Understand where the vital areas are on the animal you are hunting. Know the effective ranges and penetration capabilities of your atlatl and dart set. Always remember to represent the atlatl hobby and the sport of hunting in a positive way to others. Your conscientious, responsible behavior and professional manner will go far to leave a good impression with others in the sport, and non-hunters as well. If we take care in how hunting with the atlatl is presented we will be more likely to win acceptance for it as a viable hunting tool in every state and outside of this country as well.

Stone vs. Steel Points

Until you are able to make or find a source for stone arrowheads that are properly made and penetrate dependably, the use of modern steel game points is recommended. These are the same as those used on modern arrows. Doing this will help you get the maximum penetration needed to humanely put down the game animal.

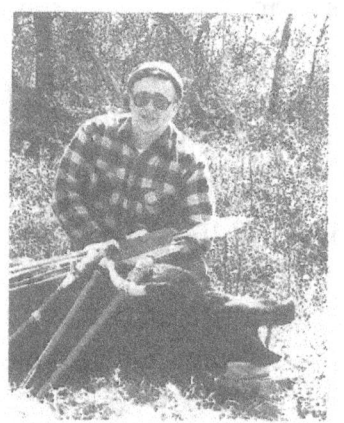

An example of how darts with steel hunting points can penetrate is found in the following account of a wild boar taken some years back. The late Lou Becker (who provided some of the designs used in the previous *Atlatl and Dart Workbook*) used a six foot dart tipped with a metal 200 grain "Jerry Hill" broadhead point. The 350 pound boar charged at him head on. The dart was thrown and hit high on the body and behind the head so hard it penetrated down and back with about 18 inches projecting from the haunches. The animal ran only about 20 yards before dropping stone cold. Anyone familiar with these wild hogs knows how tough their hides are, so this is tremendous penetrating capability.

At a game ranch near Vidalia, Georgia, the owner wanted to cull one of his bison from the herd and put it in his freezer. One dart through the lungs was enough to put it down. The dart went right through the bison from 25 yards away.

Another example is this report of an atlatl penetration study undertaken in Zimbabwe. A researcher from the University of Wyoming had permission to perform a study on elephants that had been shot and culled from the herd by game wardens. He was getting ready to spear one of the animals when it suddenly came to and got up. The dart was thrown and went in near the front leg and penetrated the lungs. The elephant immediately dropped to its knees and "keeled over". There's no doubt these things worked on mastodons and mammoths.

This is not to say that stone is incapable of good penetration. It was used prehistorically for thousands of years with great success and in the present as well. A stone hunting point is very effective if made and sharpened by a flintknapper who really knows his stuff. But again, for a person just beginning to hunt with an atlatl and darts I recommend starting with darts tipped with steel points.

Getting Close To Game

The usual advice for getting close to game applies to atlatl hunting as well. For deer you'll want to wear camo. Try using a cover scent like fox urine around your stand and on your boots. You might want to try wearing rubber boots because human scent can go through leather and the deer may pick up on it. Pay attention to wind direction. You want to be down wind of the deer. The effective distance for taking deer with an atlatl is 20 yards or under.

When hunting with an atlatl it's important to wait for only one deer to come in. If you have more than that, one or another of them will have their heads up and will be looking around. They'll catch any movement and warn the rest of the group. Also, you may want to make use of an American Indian maxim and wait for the deer to lower its head three times before you throw. The first time he puts his head down he is smelling, the second time he's tasting, the third time he is down for good. That's when you throw your dart.

Fishing With The Atlatl

Fishing brings a new dimension to an old sport for the atlatl enthusiast. Anyone who has gone bow fishing can tell you how much fun it is. With an atlatl and dart it can be even more so! Once again, before trying it you should check local fishing laws and obtain the necessary licenses.

For fishing, wooden darts will work but are apt to warp after continual use. The one-piece modern graphite dart shown in this book works great for fishing but you'll have to make a few changes to it. You won't need fletching on your fishing dart because the attached line provides the drag. If you wish to add fletching anyway, it should be made of plastic so as to be water resistant. The fishing line is of the standard bow fishing variety and is attached to the back end

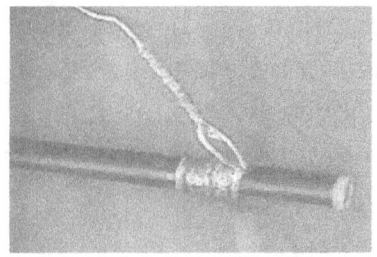

of the dart as shown in the picture on the left. Give yourself a nice amount of line so you have enough slack to cast the dart out to the target without being hindered by your line. If you are fishing from a boat you could just tie the other end of the line to it, but it's nice to use a winder. A spear point like the one shown in the photograph below can be screwed onto the end of the dart. It has retractable barbs that help keep the fish on better.

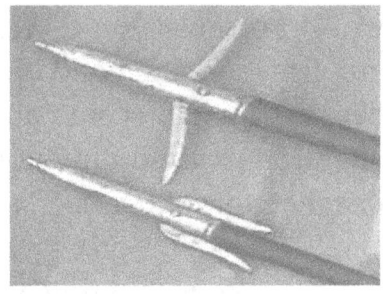

Accurate shot placement will take practice. The water causes a bit of light deflection and makes the fish look like it's at a different depth than it really is. Think of when you fill a glass up with water and then stand a pencil up in it. When you look at the part that's in the water, the pencil looks like it's shifted to the side in the glass. You'll need to take this phenomenon into account when you throw at fish. Practice will be the best teacher, but at about fifteen yards you'll probably want to try aiming six to ten inches under the fish. The amount of this correction decreases the closer the fish is to you. You may also need to lead it a bit if it's moving, but most successful shots happen when the fish aren't on the move.

In Michigan there is a season provided for spearing carp. They begin spawning in the early warmth of April and continue until the end of June. On sunny days you will see the water rolling with them but on cooler days they are more apt to be in weedier areas.

Carp are bottom feeders. If their populations are allowed to go unchecked they can cause serious problems with other fish populations. The carp muddy up the river and lake bottoms and during the time of the run, when they are gathered together in such great numbers, they destroy the eggs of game fish. This can cause game fish populations to go way down. For this reason many states try to control carp populations by allowing large numbers to be taken. There are places where huge bow fishing tournaments are held to help bring their numbers down. Atlatls can usually be used at these events as well. The fish taken at these tournaments are trucked out into the country and split up between the various farmers in the area for use as fertilizer in their fields.

ATLATL FISHING RIG

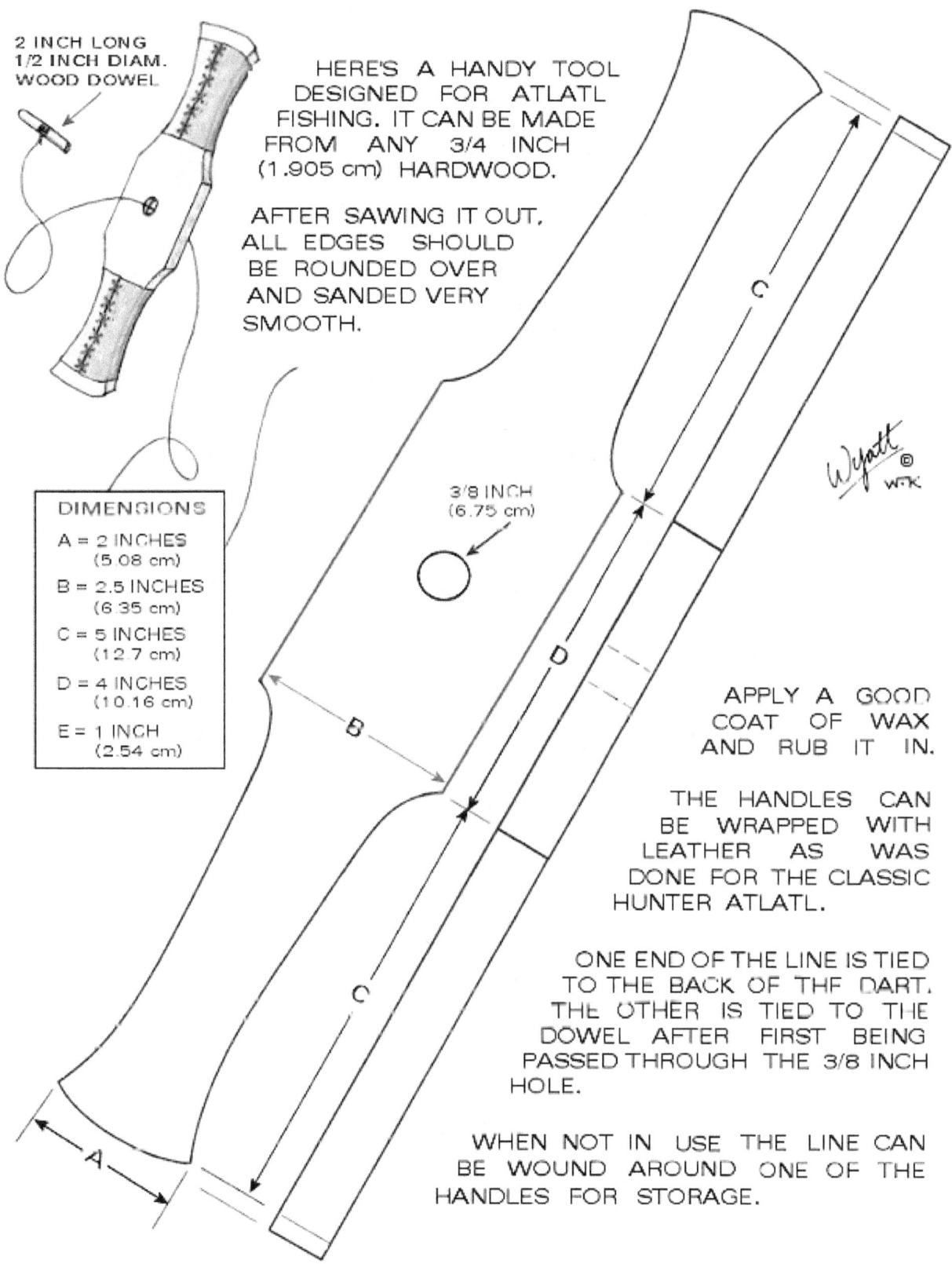

2 INCH LONG
1/2 INCH DIAM.
WOOD DOWEL

HERE'S A HANDY TOOL
DESIGNED FOR ATLATL
FISHING. IT CAN BE MADE
FROM ANY 3/4 INCH
(1.905 cm) HARDWOOD.

AFTER SAWING IT OUT,
ALL EDGES SHOULD
BE ROUNDED OVER
AND SANDED VERY
SMOOTH.

3/8 INCH
(6.75 cm)

DIMENSIONS

A = 2 INCHES
    (5.08 cm)
B = 2.5 INCHES
    (6.35 cm)
C = 5 INCHES
    (12.7 cm)
D = 4 INCHES
    (10.16 cm)
E = 1 INCH
    (2.54 cm)

APPLY A GOOD
COAT OF WAX
AND RUB IT IN.

THE HANDLES CAN
BE WRAPPED WITH
LEATHER AS WAS
DONE FOR THE CLASSIC
HUNTER ATLATL.

ONE END OF THE LINE IS TIED
TO THE BACK OF THE DART.
THE OTHER IS TIED TO THE
DOWEL AFTER FIRST BEING
PASSED THROUGH THE 3/8 INCH
HOLE.

WHEN NOT IN USE THE LINE CAN
BE WOUND AROUND ONE OF THE
HANDLES FOR STORAGE.

Firm-fleshed early season carp taken from clean water can be delicious smoked, baked or fried. Here are some favorite recipes:

SPICY DEEP FRIED FISH BATTER

2 eggs, slightly beaten
1 cup milk
2 teaspoons horseradish mustard
2 teaspoons Worcestershire sauce

1-½ cups flour
3 Tbsp. baking powder
1 teaspoon garlic salt

Pinch of cayenne pepper to taste (optional)

Beat the eggs then mix in the milk, mustard, and Worcestershire sauce. Add the dry ingredients, beating just until smooth. Deep fry until the fish is flakey. Do not over cook.

Some Hints For Deep-Frying Fish:

1. Mix the batter just until the ingredients are combined, as too much mixing can affect the baking powder action.

2. Marinate the fillets in citrus juice before applying the batter for better flavor.

3. Always pat the fillets dry before coating them with the batter.

BAKED CARP

Carp fillets cut into serving size pieces

1 cup finely crumbled bread crumbs
¼ teaspoon black pepper
¼ teaspoon cayenne pepper
½ teaspoon salt
1 teaspoon Mrs. Dash seasoning

½ cup milk
1 Tbsp. cooking oil

Mix the dry ingredients together well. Dip the fillets in milk then roll them in the seasoned mix. Place the fish in an oiled baking dish and drizzle oil lightly over each fillet. Bake at 400° for 15 minutes or until the fish flakes with a fork.

If you get a carp from clean water and it's a good firm-fleshed one from early in the season, there's no reason why you shouldn't try them on your dinner plate. When properly cleaned and put through a smoker they're delicious and their taste has been compared to "the best ham"!

Try fishing with your atlatl and darts. It's a great reason to get outdoors and enjoy your ancient skills.

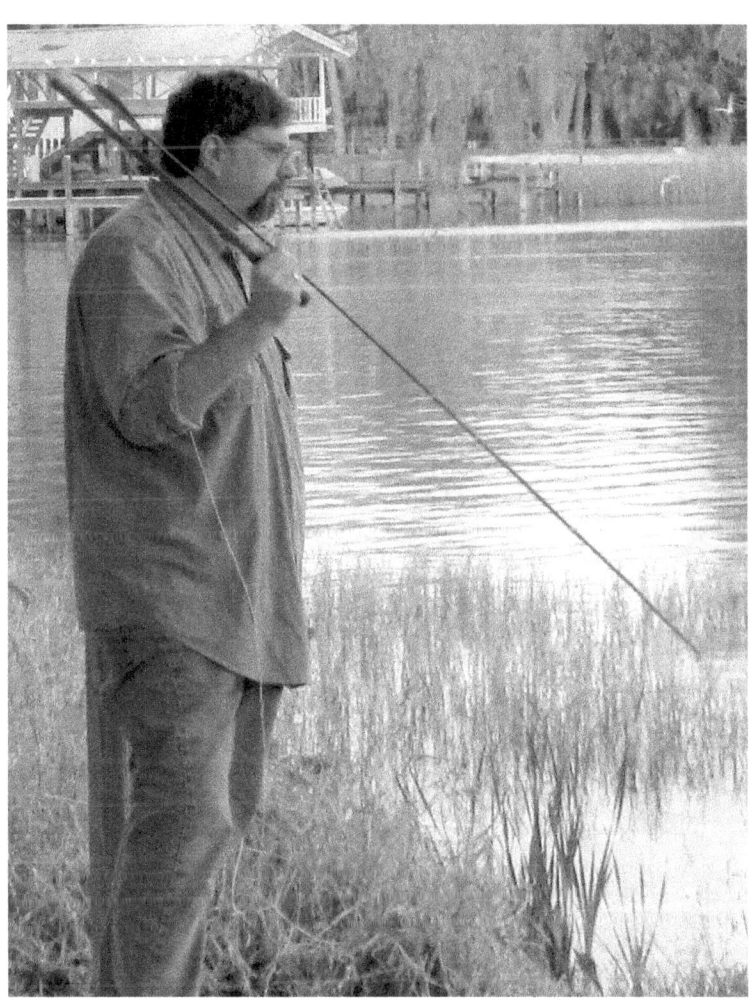

A Word From The Author…

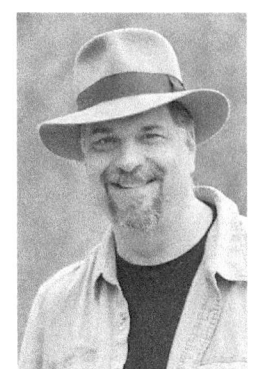

We've come a long way since the beginning of the book. You no doubt have a good understanding of atlatl and dart construction and how the system functions. You've probably built yourself an atlatl and a set of darts, and hopefully your practice is paying off. Perhaps you are thinking of competing, or hunting and fishing with your atlatl.

You may wish to build on the knowledge you've gained by researching other ideas about atlatl and dart construction that are out there. You could experiment and come up with designs of your own. Or perhaps you'd like to research more about the history of the atlatl and create museum quality reproductions. So much has been learned about atlatls over the last few decades and new discoveries are being made all the time. I believe we are in the midst of a new golden age for the atlatl.

I hope you have found this book helpful in learning about atlatls and darts and that you will continue to enjoy this fascinating and ancient sport. Share it with your children and your friends.

Good Luck!

Wyatt

APPENDIX

DART MAKING AND USAGE TIPS
Weight, Ballast, Fletching, etc.

- It's important to keep darts straight and protected from the elements when they are not in use.

- When target shooting at archery clubs, please be considerate and use darts with foreshafts no larger in diameter than conventional arrow shafts so you don't tear up the targets. Atlatl and dart usage is a sister sport to archery and respectful practices will go far to gain acceptance for it at more and more clubs.

- The balance point of a fletched dart should be about 6 to 8 inches (15.24 to 20.32cm) forward of center. All of this forward weight should not be concentrated at the tip but rather it should be evenly distributed along the front half of the dart. If you are using darts that are not fletched, the balance point is 2/3 forward of center. This makes them point heavy so you'll need to adjust your trajectory accordingly.

- A dart that balances less then the recommended 6 to 8 inches forward of center will likely need longer or larger fletching on the back of the dart. When a dart with this configuration is thrown it will exhibit more velocity at first, but it won't travel as far because of the increased drag from the larger fletching. But if you reduce the size and area of the fletching, performance will suffer as the dart will fly erratically. Adding ballast or weight at the point end in order to make the dart balance about 6 to 8 inches forward of center should increase its stability.

- Flexibility is a big deal with atlatl darts, but don't make them too floppy or performance suffers. Making them too stiff is a problem as well. Generally speaking, if the fletched end of the dart kicks down at release from the thrower, the dart's spine is too stiff. If it kicks up, it's too flexible and will need to be shortened a little bit at a time until the problem is cured. This type of "spine" testing is best done using the amount of "throwing power" you would normally apply when throwing at targets. Be sure to perform this test with darts that aren't fletched yet. The fletching is added after the dart has been "tuned".

- Try to match the width and length of the fletching to the dart style. Too much drag from the fletching can affect a dart's flight just as much as having no fletching at all.

- When making a dart out of bamboo or river cane, use the narrower end for the fletched end. This helps it to have the all-important "weight forward" requirement of good atlatl performance.

- Don't be afraid to experiment with lengths and flexibility. There's room for variation and improvement on current ideas for dart making. Australian darts are heavier, Alaskan darts used for seal hunting are shorter and lighter. Often designs reflect how tall or robust the person using them is, the environment they will be used in, and the kind of the animals being hunted.

A complete atlatl dart was found recently in a melting ice patch high in the Rocky Mountains of North America near Yellowstone National Park. At three feet long, the 10,000 year old dart was very short and lightweight compared to its modern day counterparts. Made from a birch sapling, it still had personal markings on it from the ancient hunter who once owned it.

USING SINEW

Sinew is the perfect natural material for hafting, strengthening and securing many traditional or Paleo projects. It has been used for thousands of years in the making of bows, bow strings, knives, tools, clothing items, etc. It's authentic, extremely strong, wear resistant, and easy to use.

Sinew can be obtained from a variety of animals including moose, elk and caribou. However, backstrap and leg sinew from deer is often more readily available. Leg sinew is a whitish cord that runs the length of the lower leg. I prefer backstrap sinew which comes out as flatter sheets that are teased apart into strands. Leg or backstrap sinew can be obtained from hunters, deer processors, or butchers. It is also available from hide and fur sellers. (See Source List in the Appendix on Page 84.)

If you get fresh sinew, you'll need to prepare it for use, which means it will need to be cleaned and dried. Carefully scrape it until all the meat, fat, etc. is off and you have only sinew left. But take it easy! You don't want to cut into the

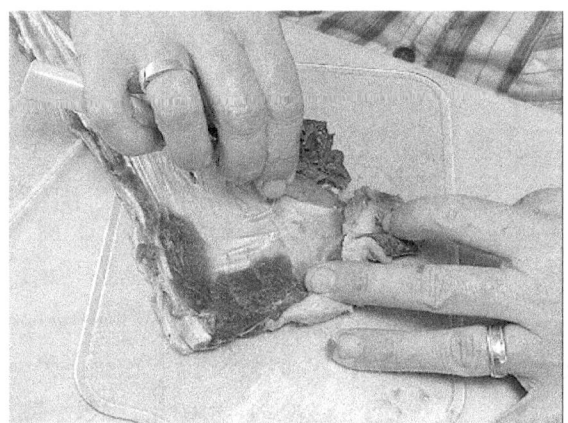 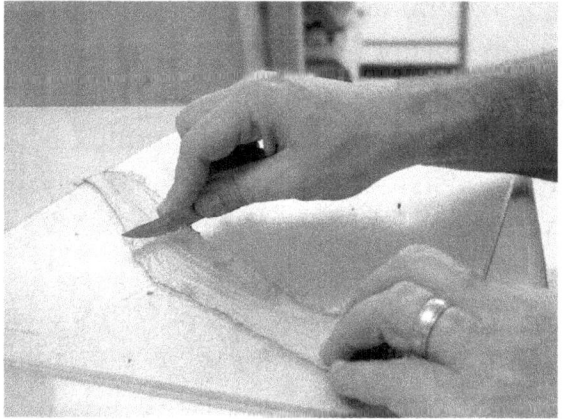

Scraping backstrap sinew

sinew itself. On backstrap sinew you'll find that one side is covered with a thin membrane or "fascia". It's best to remove as much of this fascia as possible. After you've cleaned the sinew, lay it out on a rack or board to dry thoroughly. Once it's dry (depending on conditions it could take a couple of days) you'll need to keep it that way, so you should store it in a water tight container or large plastic re-sealable zipper storage bag.

When you have need of it for a project, the dried sinew must be separated into thin strands. As mentioned above, backstrap sinew can be pulled or teased apart. Leg sinew, on the other hand, requires special treatment. Find a hard surface like the top of your work bench and use a flat-bottomed stone or wooden mallet to lightly pound the sinew from end to end, making sure to keep the face of the mallet parallel to the sinew. Keep pounding until you see it separate into thin strands. I once saw strands of sinew referred to as looking like "dental floss"--a very apt description.

When you're ready to use the sinew, take as many strands as you feel you'll need and keep them moistened in a shallow container of water. When hafting, or joining two pieces together, hide glue is used in conjunction with the sinew. Get a small container and warm some hide glue to the point of melting. A little pan over a hot plate, double boiler, a Sterno® burner, or even a candle flame can be used. Keep it just warm

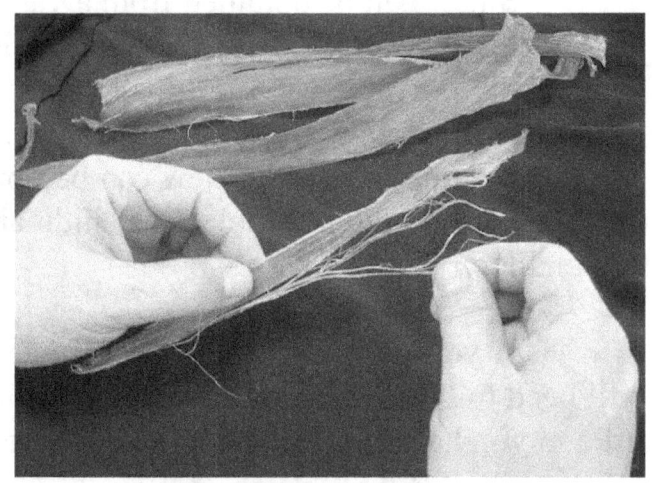

Pulling off strands of backstrap sinew

enough to stay liquid, but not so hot that it will burn your fingers while you use it. (If you run out of hide glue or have trouble finding it, you can use Knox® Unflavored Gelatin as a substitute. Mix a packet with enough tepid water to make it the consistency of thin pancake syrup and use it the same as real hide glue. I have used it with excellent results.)

Take a strand of sinew and coat it by dipping it in the hide glue. Use your fingers to wipe off the excess glue and carefully apply the wraps to your project. Don't pull the sinew too tight while it's wet or it will break. Set your project aside to dry. Sometimes it can take up to 24 hours to dry fully.

After the sinew has dried you'll find it will have shrunk, and in the process it will have pulled everything together very tightly. Once dry, the sinew wraps should be coated with wax or varnish to keep them water proof, as they will come apart if they get wet again.

WRAPPING WITH SINEW

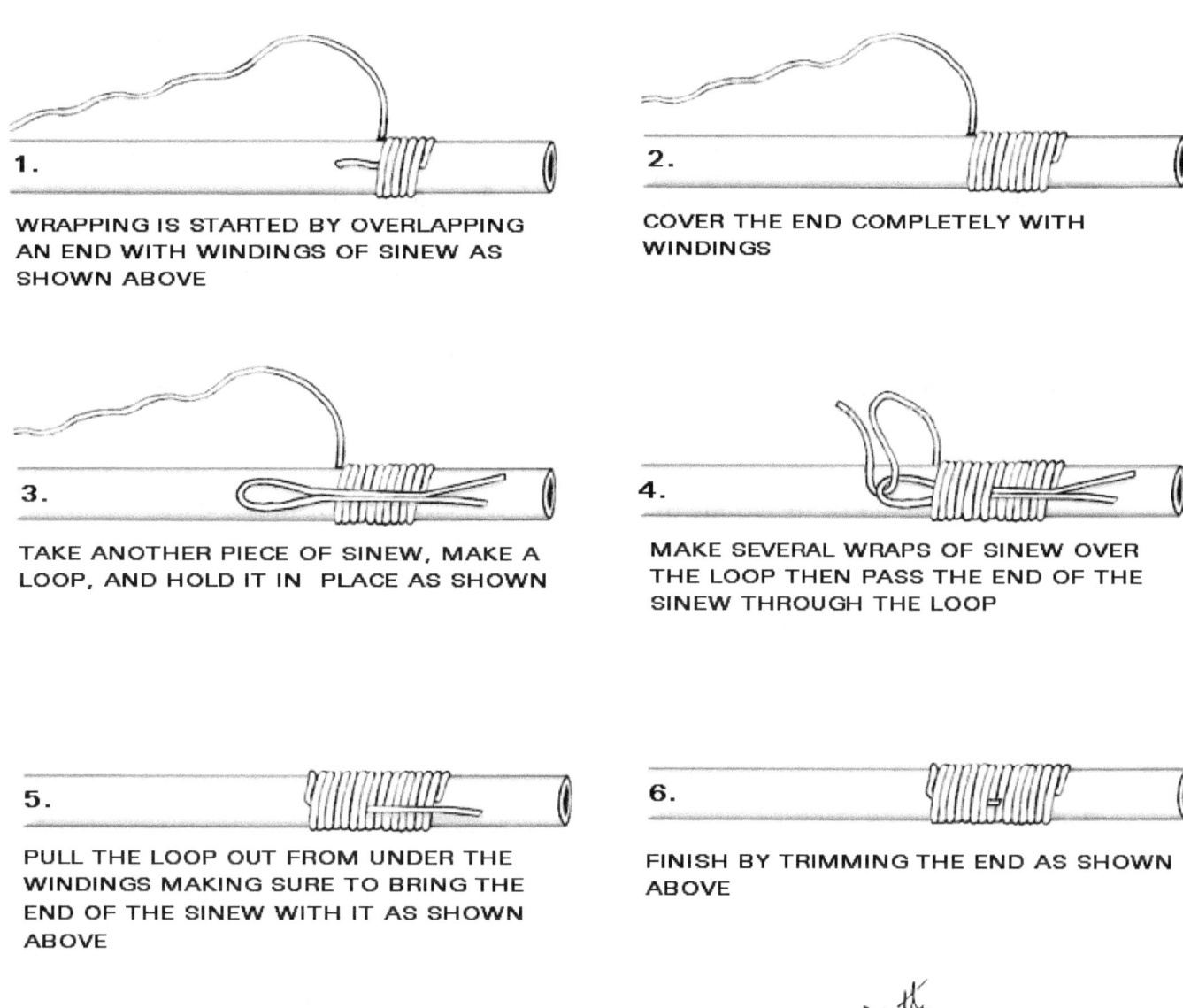

1.

WRAPPING IS STARTED BY OVERLAPPING AN END WITH WINDINGS OF SINEW AS SHOWN ABOVE

2.

COVER THE END COMPLETELY WITH WINDINGS

3.

TAKE ANOTHER PIECE OF SINEW, MAKE A LOOP, AND HOLD IT IN PLACE AS SHOWN

4.

MAKE SEVERAL WRAPS OF SINEW OVER THE LOOP THEN PASS THE END OF THE SINEW THROUGH THE LOOP

5.

PULL THE LOOP OUT FROM UNDER THE WINDINGS MAKING SURE TO BRING THE END OF THE SINEW WITH IT AS SHOWN ABOVE

6.

FINISH BY TRIMMING THE END AS SHOWN ABOVE

ADDING FINGER LOOPS

Many atlatl enthusiasts add finger loops to their atlatls in order to provide a more secure and consistently placed grip. If you would like to add them to your atlatl you can use a method much the same as was used prehistorically in North America.

Begin by cutting strips from soft tanned deerskin or other hide according to the pattern below. The loops are then made by sliding the "cross cut" in the strips over the tip end of the atlatl and then down to the handle end where they stop against either the leather handle wrap or a preplanned larger handle diameter. The ends of the strips are then brought back forward and secured to the atlatl shaft with sinew. Before applying the sinew wraps, test the fit of the loops and adjust the length accordingly by locating the ends farther forward or backward on the atlatl shaft. The pictures on Page 81 will help you see how it all comes together.

There are many variations of this method -- don't be afraid to experiment. For instance, another way to make the loops would be to make a one-piece pattern as shown at the bottom of Page 81. Measurements are the same except the length would be 14 inches (35.56 cm). You could also try braided finger loops. The ancient Aztecs even made finger loops from shells!

FINGER LOOP PATTERN
(MAKE TWO)

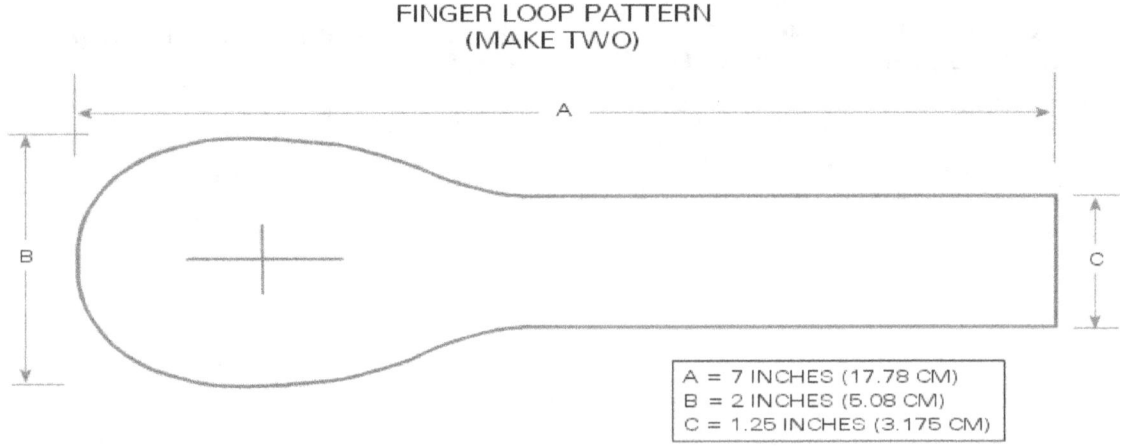

A = 7 INCHES (17.78 CM)
B = 2 INCHES (5.08 CM)
C = 1.25 INCHES (3.175 CM)

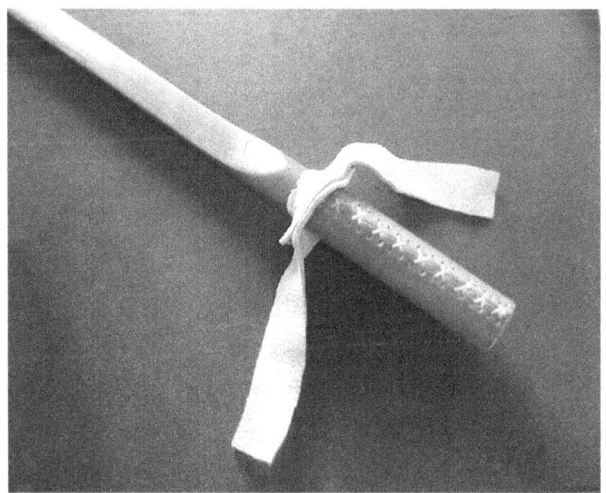

The strips in place on the atlatl shaft prior to lashing the ends down with sinew.

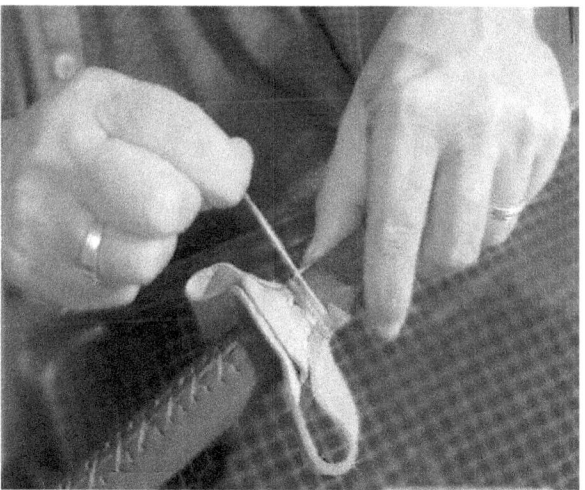

The loops being secured in place on the atlatl shaft with sinew wraps.

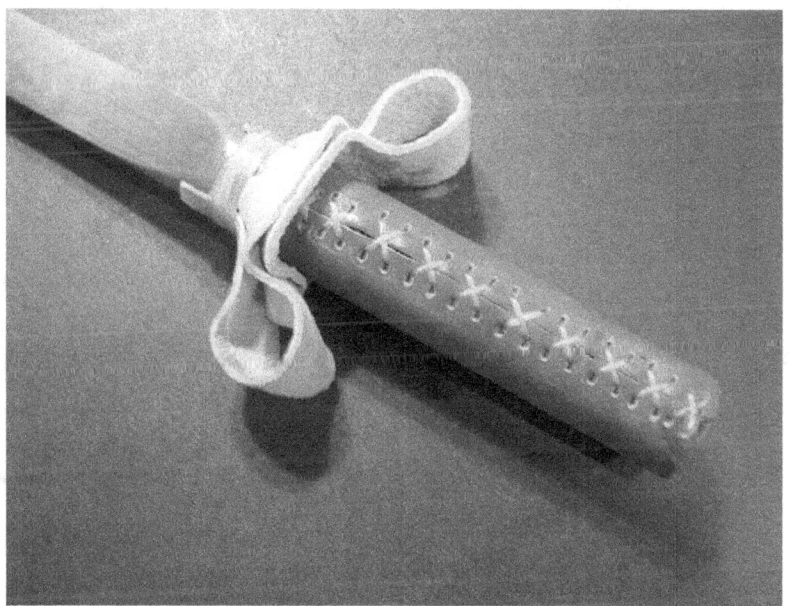

The finished loops.

ALTERNATE FINGER LOOP PATTERN
(MAKE ONE)

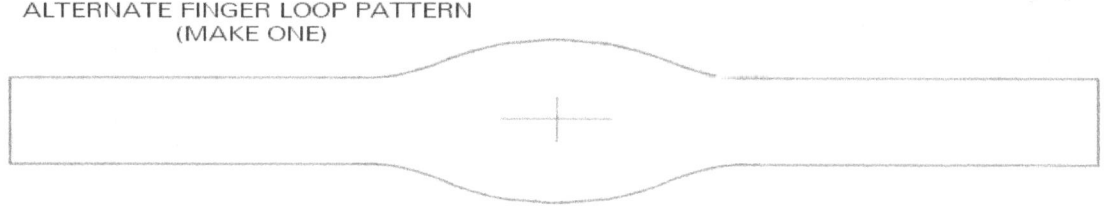

HAFTING STONE POINTS WITH PITCH AND SINEW

Great satisfaction can be found using traditional materials and methods to haft stone points. Pitch and sinew hafting is authentic, looks great, and the resulting bond between stone and shaft is extremely strong. (The recipe for pine pitch hafting glue can be found on Page 32.)

Before getting started, there are some things you need to know. When heating pitch it is important to work in a well-ventilated place. It is best to use an indirect heat source such as coals from a fire, however if you are careful, the flame from a camp stove or a Sterno® burner will work. Don't let the pitch get so hot that it starts dripping or catches on fire. It should be just soft enough to get a bit of pitch off the pitch stick and into the notch of the shaft--the heat from the stone tip will do the rest.

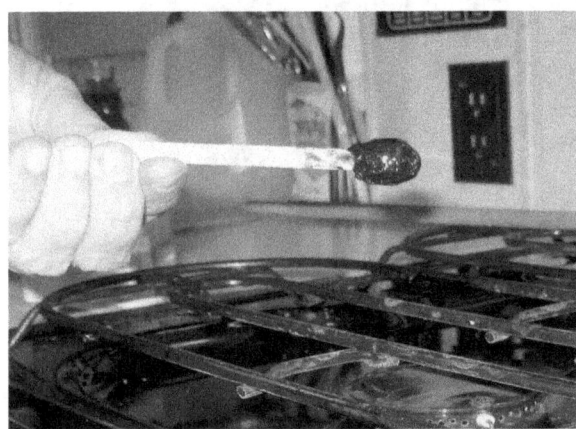

Heating the pitch

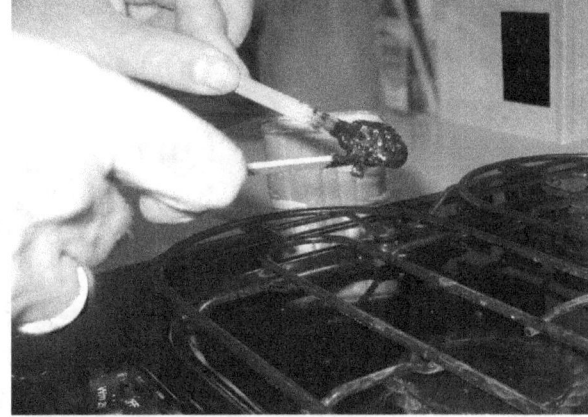

Getting a bit of softened pitch off the pitch stick to fill the notch of the shaft

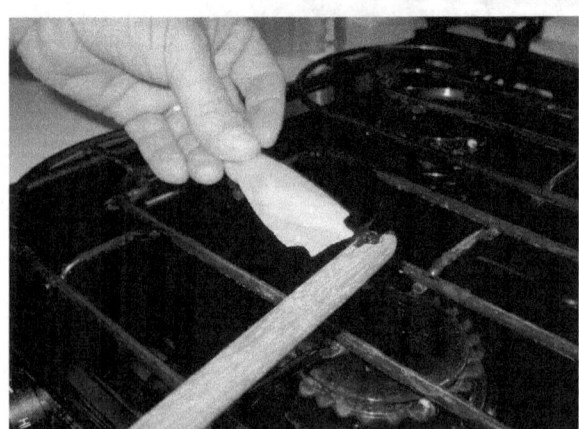

Heating the stone point

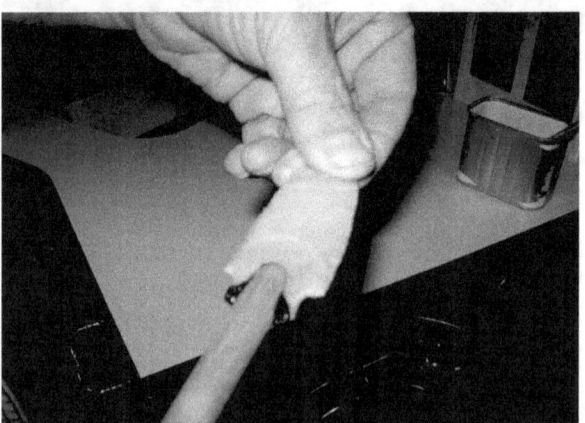

Seating the point in the pitch-filled notch (and holding it in proper alignment until it cools)

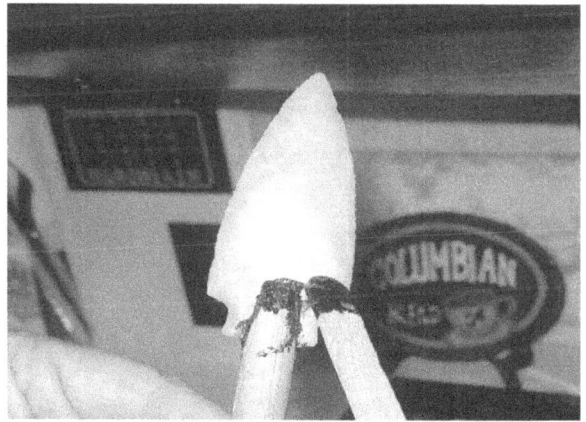

Filling in the gaps (The notch was cut slightly wider than the point in order to get a stronger bond from the pitch glue.)

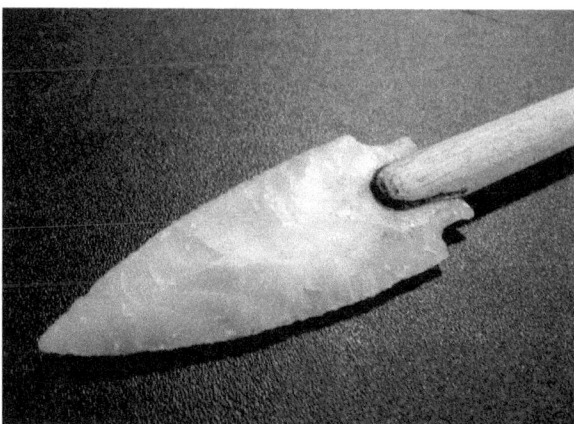

Excess pitch is scraped off the point and the shaft. The remaining pitch is smoothed with a hot knife

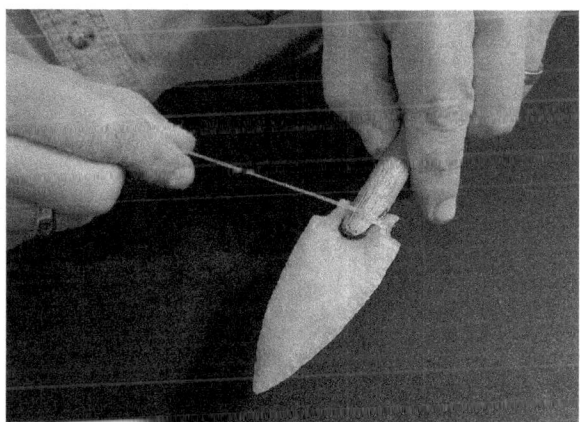

Applying sinew wraps (See Pages 77-78) The sharp edges of the hafting area were abraded to prevent the sinew from being cut as it dried.

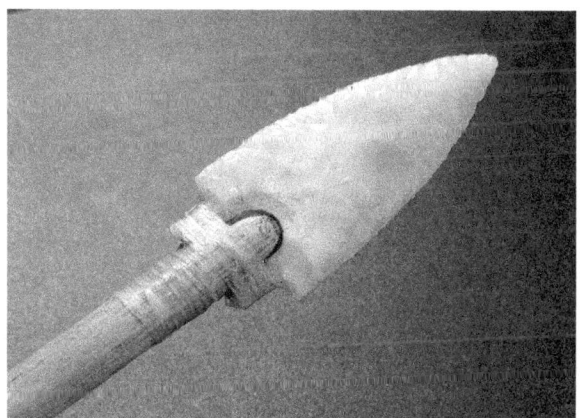

The finished hafted point

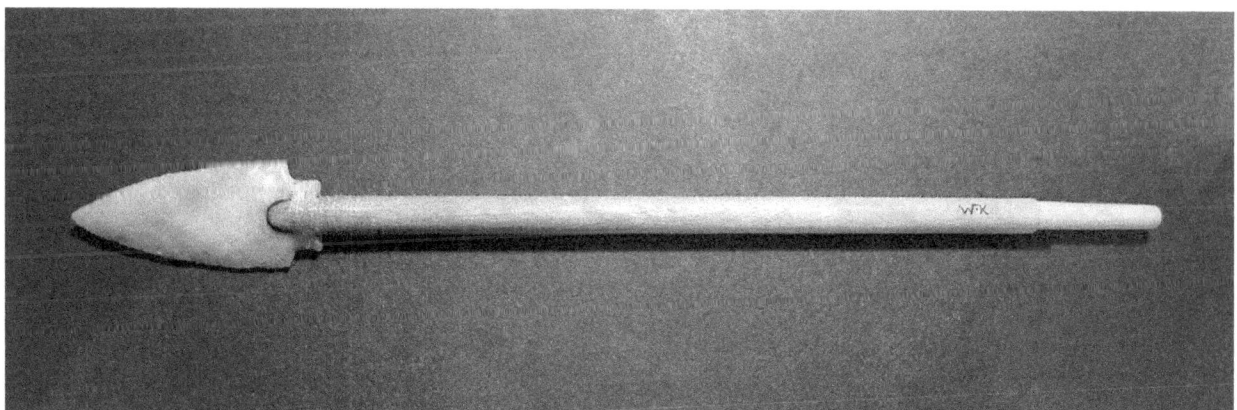

An authentically hafted dart foreshaft

MATERIALS SOURCE LIST

The following materials resource list is provided in case you are unable to find what you need at your local archery supply, leather, or hardware and lumber outlets.

GLUES, CRESTING & DIPPING LAQUERS

BOHNING ADHESIVES CO., LTD.
7361 NORTH 7 MILE ROAD
LAKE CITY, MI 49651
PHONE: (231) 229-4247

WILD TURKEY FEATHERS FOR DARTS

CUSTOM FEATHERS
6117 HIGHWAY 190
CHILLICOTHE, MO 64601
PHONE: (888) 353-8246

GOLD TIP® CARBON FIBER SHAFTING & ARROW COMPONENTS

368 SOUTH GOLD TIP DRIVE
OREM, UT 84058
PHONE: (800) 551-0541
www.goldtip.com

SINEW, ANTLER, BONE, LEATHER, HIDE GLUE & FEATHERS

MOSCOW HIDE AND FUR
P.O. BOX 8918
MOSCOW, ID 83843
PHONE: (208) 882-0601
www.hideandfur.com

RIVER CANE SHAFTING

You can look for it at flintknapping or primitive archery events. You can find it growing from about the middle of Kentucky on down south to Florida. If you are having trouble finding some, try the following source:

MIKE McGUIRE
ROUTE 1, BOX 126D
SPENCER, TN 38585

ATLATL WEIGHTS & PALEO ATLATL REPLICAS

Beautiful replica atlatls and atlatl weights made from correct materials, and also resin cast replicas of rare Paleolithic ivory and antler atlatls from Europe can be admired and even purchased from the following source:

OCCOQUAN PALEOTECHNICS
MICHAEL FRANK
3019 BROMLEY COURT
WOODBRIDGE, VA 22192
http://www.occpaleo.com/

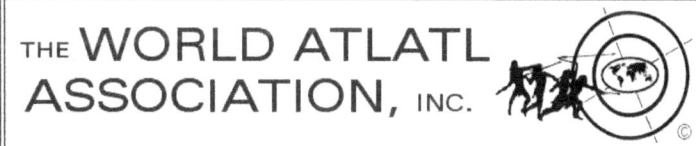

Following you will find an overview of the ISAC rules for competition and safety as set forth by the World Atlatl Association at the time of publication of this book. For a complete listing of the most current WAA rules and policies, consult the World Atlatl Association website at:

http://www.worldatlatl.org/ISACrules.html

WORLD ATLATL ASSOCIATION STANDARD ACCURACY CONTEST (ISAC Rules)
Revised 17 November 2006

The purpose of these rules is to provide contests that will be as identical as possible no matter when or where they take place. This degree of standardization makes it possible for atlatlists to compare their ability with others around the world without having face to face competition. The contest will also be used to identify the most accurate atlatlists in the world for any given year. Contestants are encouraged to compete several times during the year using either Primitive or Open Equipment. The highest score thrown during the year will be used for ranking purposes. Men and women of all ages will compete in the same contest. The WAA may, at its own discretion, make separate awards based on age, gender, and type of equipment used. Since this is a year long contest, the WAA will present any awards at the end of the throwing year. To aid people in the interpretation of these rules and to help ensure that contests are as identical as possible, a statement of intent has been attached to these rules (Appendix A)

1 TARGET

1.1 The target used is a bulls-eye target having the following dimensions: X-ring 10.0 cm diameter 10-ring 24.0 cm diameter 9-ring 40.0 cm diameter 8-ring 56.0 cm diameter 7-ring 80.0 cm diameter 6-ring 108.0 cm diameter. The total dimensions of the target must be large enough that there will be at least 5 cm of space between the 6-ring and the edge of the target.

1.2 The area between the X- and 10 rings is to be black to form the bullseye. The area of the X-ring may be left uncolored or, optionally, may be painted any color desired. The coloring of both the x- and 10-rings must be done in such a way that the compass lines used to mark the rings are still visible. This is necessary for precise scoring.

1.3 A target may be used without a backstop such as hay bales or similar materials. With this usage the holes in the target are to be patched with tape at the end of each round of throwing.

1.4 The target is to be placed so the center of the bullseye is between 80 and 110 cm above the surface of the ground.

2 EQUIPMENT

2.1 There are two classifications of equipment: Primitive and Open.

2.2 For Primitive equipment, both the atlatl and the darts must be made of natural materials that would have been available to prehistoric people. Copper points are considered to be primitive.

2.2a Modern glues and artificial sinew are exceptions to above rule 2.2.

2.2b   The maximum diameter of the dart, including the point but excepting the fletching, must not exceed 19.0mm (.748 in). In other words, the unfletched dart would pass through a ring having a 19.0mm inside diameter.

2.2c   The contest organizers are required to have on hand a suitable 19.0 mm gauge to ensure that dart diameters are consistent with rule 2.2b.

2.3   There are no restrictions on material or design for Open equipment except that rule 2.2b applies to Open equipment.

2.4   The same atlatl and dart must be used throughout the contest.

2.4a   If equipment is broken during a throw, it may be replaced and the contestant will be allowed to repeat the throw.

2.4b   An exception to rule 2.4a is that if a contestant deliberately breaks his own equipment by throwing it, slamming it into the ground, or similar unsportsman like behavior, the equipment will not be replaced and the contestant must leave the contest immediately.

3 DISTANCES

3.1   The complete contest consists of ten consecutive throws, five throws each from 15 and 20 meters distance for a total of ten.

3.1a   The 15 meter portion of the contest will be thrown first.

3.2   The throwing distance must be clearly marked by a line at least three meters long.

3.2a   If a contestant steps on or over the line while throwing, any score from that throw will not count towards the total.

4 CONDUCT OF THE CONTEST

4.1   The WAA guidelines on safety and behavior apply to this contest.

4.2   Each flight must have a designated score keeper before beginning to throw.

4.3   In each round the contestants are to throw in turn a single dart at the target. At the end of each round the contestants will rotate so that the contestant that was first the previous round will move to the last position and the contestant that was second will move to first and so on for each round. At the end of five rounds, each member of a five man flight will have thrown from each position in the rotation.

4.4   The size of a flight allowed to throw at a single target during a round shall not exceed five contestants nor contain less than three contestants.

4.4a   When there is more than one flight, the contestants are to be divided so that the flights are as equal in size as possible.

4.4b   If a contestant is removed from a three man flight for either unsafe or disruptive behavior, the remaining members of the flight will finish the contest by alternating turns of throwing first.

4.5   No darts are to be removed from the target during a round until all of the members of a flight have thrown their dart.

4.5a   An exception to rule 4.5 is that the score keeper may allow the removal of a dart that has stuck at such an angle from the perpendicular that it is in danger of being broken by subsequent throws.

4.5b   A dart that is reasonably parallel to a line between the target and the throwing line is not to be removed regardless of its position in the target.

4.5c   The score keeper is the final judge of whether or not a dart can be pulled before all members of a flight have thrown to complete the round.

4.6   The contestants are not to touch or remove any dart from the target until authorized by the score keeper.

4.7   Contest organizers are to ensure that additional targets are available if needed to replace those that have become hard to score due to taking many hits.

4.8   A contestant is limited to participating in the World Atlatl Association Standard Accuracy Contest only one time during a given day. Re-entry type contests where a competitor is allowed to repeat a contest several times during the same day are specifically forbidden.

5 SCORING

5.1   To score the dart must either stick, distal end first, or pass through the target.

5.2   The score for a given throw is based on the highest scoring area touched by the hole in the target.

5.3   No score is given for hits that do not at least touch the 6-ring.

5.4   The scorekeeper is the final judge of the score given for any throw.

5.4a   Any dart that ricochets off of the ground before hitting the target will be scored a miss.

5.4b   If a thrower "miscues" by letting a dart slip off of the spur while throwing and the dart travels far enough that the back end of the dart is more than 2.0 meters from the throwing line it will be counted as a "throw" and scored accordingly.

5.4c   If a thrown dart sticks into the nock, however briefly, of a dart already sticking in the target, and is effectively blocked from reaching the target, the throw will be given the same score as the dart that was struck. This procedure will be used whether or not the thrown dart actually sticks in the nock of the dart already in the target or merely hits in the nock but fails to stick and falls to the ground. The key is that the second dart was blocked from reaching the target.

5.4d   Any dart that ricochets off of darts already sticking in the target before itself sticking into the target will be scored on the basis of where it hits the target.

5.5   In case of a tie, the contestant having the most "X's" will be declared the winner.

5.5a   If the tie is not broken by rule 5.5 the contestant having the most hits scoring ten will be declared the winner. If the tie still is not broken, the contestant with the most nines will be declared the winner. This process will continue using the most eights, and then the most sevens until the tie is broken.

5.5b   If rule 5.5a does not break the tie the contestants will be declared co-winners.

THE WORLD ATLATL ASSOCIATION SAFETY GUIDELINES
Revised January 2005

The atlatl and dart is a weapon system designed initially for hunting and should be considered dangerous. Because there is a potential for injury through atlatl use, The World Atlatl Association has found it necessary to adopt certain safety guidelines for all atlatl events. These guidelines are designed so as not to interfere with the prime purpose of these events, which is fun, demonstration, and education. Because atlatl events are held in different locations with special restrictions due to terrain features or other reasons, an all-encompassing set of rules may not be possible. Safety officials, event sponsors, event organizers, or others may supplement the following with special guidelines that apply to their local situation.

GENERAL GUIDELINES: Safety officers should be designated for every atlatl event and authorized to enforce the guidelines. Safety guidelines should be followed not only during competition, but also in instructional and non-competitive situations as well. Safety decisions by safety officers take precedence over those of scorekeepers, instructors, and participants. Safety officers may, at any time, remove from the field anyone who does not adhere to these guidelines. Prior to the start of the atlatl event, the safety officers should explain the safety guidelines to all participants and determine that spectators are behind the safety line established for each contest. When more than one group is in the field, the scorekeeper for each group is authorized to act as safety officer for his/her group and has the authority to enforce these guidelines. Only participants (throwers, scorekeepers, and safety officers) should be allowed on the field during contests, demonstrations, or practice. Exceptions may be made for news media or others, but each exception should be approved by the safety officer. Pets are not allowed on the field during contests, practice, or demonstration. There should never be rowdy or unruly play with atlatls and darts at any time during or after the contest while on the throwing field. To prevent injury to the thrower or others on the field, darts should be carried vertically (points down). No person should ever be running with darts in hand. The prime guidelines for atlatl safety are: do not throw when others are down range and do not throw or retrieve darts until the scorekeeper gives permission to do so. These guidelines should be universal in atlatl events.

GUIDELINES FOR SPECIFIC TYPE CONTESTS: WAA Target Round, American Field Round, European Style: These contests employ multiple targets and throwing lines at various throwing distances and require extra caution when sending groups to the throwing line to begin a round. Starting a group should be timed/spaced in order to avoid contestants throwing when another group is in line with any target on either side of their intended target. Targets should not be placed in line or in close proximity to other targets. Darts should not be thrown or retrieved from a target until all persons in the group have thrown at that particular target and permission given to do so by the scorekeeper. When a contestant steps to the throwing line to throw, all other persons in the group should be at a safe distance

90

behind the thrower until the throw is complete. Ohio Standard Accuracy, ISAC: These contests employ multiple throwing lines for a single target. All darts should be retrieved from the target prior to throwing from another throwing line. To safely manage a group of throwers, the number should be limited to five or six, and the full course of throws should be completed prior to starting another group. Again, no darts should be thrown or retrieved without being specifically authorized by the scorekeeper. Clearly, no set of rules can encompass every possibility that may arise. It is therefore imperative that all participants and spectators follow any additional requirements that the safety officer may deem necessary for the safety of everyone involved.

TERMS:

Atlatl:	A rigid device used to propel a dart. (A spearthrower)
Dart:	A lightweight spear designed to be propelled by an atlatl.
Field:	A designated area where contests, demonstrations, or practice may be held and darts may be thrown.
Range:	That portion of the field where targets are set up for competition, demonstration, or practice.
Target:	Any specially designed point or object at which darts are thrown. Usually these are painted cardboard sheets attached to hay bales, but may be three-dimensional animal shapes, marked circles or lines on the ground, or other designated points.
Safety Line:	A designated line, whether marked or not, beyond which spectators and/or others not currently and directly involved in the atlatl event are restricted. This line may be marked by colored tape.
Throwing Line:	A designated line, usually marked with colored tape, at a prescribed distance from its corresponding target.
Safety Officer:	A person specifically designated to ensure these guidelines are observed and to oversee general safety on the atlatl field.
Scorekeeper:	A person designated to keep score and enforce these guidelines within his/her group of throwers.

You can get information on how to join the World Atlatl Association and download a Membership Application at the following web address:

http://www.worldatlatl.org/membership.html

ABOUT THE AUTHOR

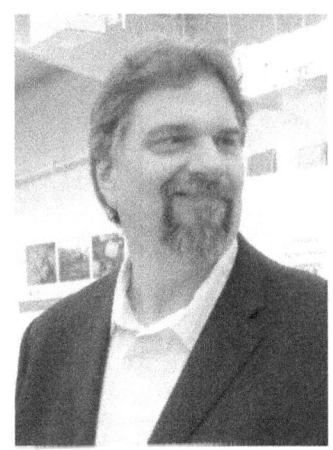

WYATT R. KNAPP is an author, illustrator, artist and musician. All his life he has enjoyed a passion for primitive skills, history and the outdoors. As a young boy he devoured the *Ben Hunt Indian Craft Books* and made as many of the projects as he could.

He later attended *Grand Valley State Colleges* in Michigan where he majored in drawing and sculpture, and further explored his interest in both history and anthropology. It was there he first heard of Ishi, the last Yahi Indian, and knew there was still hope that he could find information on how to make stone arrowheads.

Wyatt is a member of the *Michigan Flintknappers* and the *World Atlatl Association.* He has been published online as well as in various books and newspapers. He is the author of the website *"The History And Primitive Technology Page"* which was one of the select few to be featured in an article on primitive skills which appeared in *Natural History Magazine.* He wrote an ongoing column and feature articles for the *Michigan Flintknappers Newsletter.* Wyatt's publications have been used in colleges and university courses. His books have sold in the United States and Europe, as well as in countries such as Australia, Belgium and China.

Wyatt resides with his wife Shari in West Michigan and Florida where they spend much of their time working as musicians in the singing duo *"Reclaim".* When Wyatt is not working on music or writing he spends his time flintknapping, shooting his flintlock muzzleloaders and exploring primitive skills.

To order copies of this book contact us at the following address for current pricing and shipping information:

ATLATL BOOK
ONAGOCAG PUBLISHING
P.O. BOX 836
DOUGLAS, MI 49406

Or visit us on the web at: *www.onagocag.com/bookorder.html*